HOW TO START AND RUN YOUR OWN VIDEO PRODUCTION COMPANY

Gain Visibility, Engagement and Promote your Digital Production Company

Jeanelle K. Douglas

Copyright © 2024 by Jeanelle K. Douglas. All rights reserved. No part of this book, *HOW TO START AND RUN YOUR OWN VIDEO PRODUCTION COMPANY, may be reproduced, stored in a retrieval system, or transmitted in any form or by any means, electronic, mechanical, photocopying, recording, or otherwise, without the prior written permission of the author, Jeanelle K. Douglas.*

Contents

INTRODUCTION TO STARTING A VIDEO PRODUCTION COMPANY 7

    Understanding the Video Production Industry 9

    Why Start Your Own Company? 12

MARKET RESEARCH AND ANALYSIS 15

    Identifying Your Target Audience 17

    Analyzing Competitors 19

    Assessing Market Trends and Demands 22

CREATING A BUSINESS PLAN 25

    Defining Your Company's Vision and Mission 28

    Setting Objectives and Goals 30

    Developing a Revenue Model 32

    Crafting a Marketing and Sales Strategy 35

LEGAL CONSIDERATIONS AND BUSINESS STRUCTURE 38

    Choosing a Business Structure (e.g., Sole Proprietorship, LLC, Corporation) 41

    Registering Your Business and Obtaining Necessary Permits .. 43

    Understanding Copyright and Intellectual Property Laws 46

    Drafting Contracts and Agreements 49

FINANCIAL MANAGEMENT ... 52
Estimating Startup Costs ... 55
Securing Funding (if necessary) ... 58
Budgeting for Equipment, Software, and Personnel ... 61
Setting Pricing Strategies ... 64

Equipment And Technology ... 67
Selecting Cameras, Lenses, and Accessories ... 70
Investing in Editing Software and Hardware ... 73
Building a Post-Production Setup ... 76
Exploring Specialized Equipment (e.g., Drones, Stabilizers) ... 80

BUILDING YOUR TEAM ... 83
Hiring Key Personnel (e.g., Videographers, Editors, Producers) ... 86
Freelancers vs. Full-time Employees ... 89
Cultivating a Creative and Collaborative Work Environment ... 91

FINDING CLIENTS AND PROJECTS ... 94
Networking within the Industry ... 97

UTILIZING ONLINE PLATFORMS AND SOCIAL MEDIA ... 100
Pitching Your Services to Potential Clients ... 103
Establishing Long-term Client Relationships ... 106

PROJECT MANAGEMENT 109
    Planning and Scheduling Shoots 111
    Managing Resources and Logistics 113
    Overseeing Production and Post-Production Processes 115
    Ensuring Quality Control 117
MARKETING AND BRANDING 120
    Developing a Strong Brand Identity 122
    Creating a Portfolio of Work 125
    Implementing Digital Marketing Strategies (e.g., SEO, Content Marketing) 128
    Leveraging Testimonials and Case Studies 131
SCALING YOUR BUSINESS 134
    Expanding Service Offerings (e.g., Live Streaming, Animation) 137
    Scaling Operations and Infrastructure 139
    Diversifying Revenue Streams 142
    Evaluating Growth Opportunities 145
MAINTAINING SUCCESS AND SUSTAINABILITY 148
    Staying Updated with Industry Trends and Technology 151
    Continuing Education and Skill Development 154

Nurturing Client Relationships and Repeat Business 156

Adapting to Changing Market Conditions 159

CONCLUSION 162

INTRODUCTION TO STARTING A VIDEO PRODUCTION COMPANY

Starting a video production company is an exciting endeavor that allows you to unleash your creativity while fulfilling the growing demand for high-quality visual content. In today's digital age, videos have become an essential tool for businesses, brands, and individuals to communicate their messages effectively to a wide audience.

The video production industry in the United States is thriving, with a constant need for diverse content across various platforms, including television, online streaming services, social media, and corporate presentations. As businesses increasingly recognize the power of video in engaging their target audience, the demand for professional video production services continues to soar.

Embarking on the journey of starting your own video production company offers numerous opportunities for growth and success.

Whether you're a seasoned videographer looking to take control of your career or a creative entrepreneur with a passion for storytelling, launching a video production business allows you to turn your passion into a profitable venture.

However, venturing into the world of video production requires more than just technical expertise. It involves careful planning, strategic decision-making, and a deep understanding of both the creative and business aspects of the industry. From crafting compelling narratives to managing budgets and timelines, every aspect of running a successful video production company requires dedication, skill, and attention to detail.

Moreover, starting a video production company offers the freedom to pursue projects that align with your interests and values. Whether you specialize in commercial advertising, documentary filmmaking, event coverage, or corporate video production, you have the flexibility to tailor your services to cater to your target market's specific needs.

In addition to the creative rewards, running your own video production company allows you to build lasting relationships with clients and collaborators while making a meaningful impact through your work. Whether you're helping businesses tell their brand story, capturing life's special moments, or shedding light on important social issues, the ability to evoke emotions and inspire action through video is a privilege that comes with great responsibility.

As you embark on this journey, remember that success in the video production industry is not solely measured by financial gains but also by the impact you make on your clients and audience. By delivering exceptional quality, staying true to your vision, and continuously honing your craft, you can build a reputation as a trusted partner and storyteller in the ever-evolving landscape of video production.

Understanding the Video Production Industry

To thrive in the video production industry, it's essential to have a deep understanding of its dynamics, trends, and key players. At its core, the industry revolves around the creation, editing, and distribution of video content for various purposes, including entertainment, advertising, education, and communication.

One of the defining features of the video production industry is its adaptability to technological advancements and shifting consumer preferences. From traditional television broadcasts to online streaming platforms and social media channels, the ways in which people consume video content have evolved significantly over the years, presenting both challenges and opportunities for industry professionals.

Moreover, the rise of digital technology has democratized video production, allowing individuals and businesses of all sizes to create high-quality content with relatively affordable equipment and software. This democratization has led to a proliferation of content creators, resulting in a highly competitive landscape where differentiation and innovation are key to success.

Another important aspect of the video production industry is its interdisciplinary nature, drawing talent from various fields, including filmmaking, photography, graphic design, and marketing. Collaboration and teamwork are essential components of successful video production projects, requiring effective communication, creativity, and technical expertise to bring ideas to life.

The video production industry is heavily influenced by consumer trends, cultural shifts, and economic factors. Understanding these trends and anticipating future developments can help businesses stay ahead of the curve and capitalize on emerging opportunities. For example, the growing popularity of short-form video content on platforms like Tik- Tok and Instagram has prompted many businesses to invest in micro-content strategies to engage younger audiences.

In addition to creativity and technical skill, successful video production companies must also possess strong business acumen to navigate the complexities of the industry. This includes strategic planning, financial management, marketing, and client relationship management. Building a reputable brand and fostering long-term partnerships with clients and collaborators are crucial for sustained success in a competitive market.

Ultimately, the video production industry is a dynamic and ever-evolving ecosystem that offers boundless opportunities for creative expression, professional growth, and business innovation. By staying informed, adaptable, and proactive, industry professionals can thrive in this exciting and fast-paced environment, creating impactful content that resonates with audiences around the world.

Why Start Your Own Company?

Starting your own company offers a multitude of benefits and opportunities that may not be readily available in traditional employment settings.

Here are several compelling reasons why individuals choose to start their own companies:

1. Independence and Autonomy: Starting your own company allows you to be your own boss, make decisions independently, and chart your own course. You have the freedom to set your own goals, priorities, and work schedule, providing a greater sense of control over your professional life.

2. Pursuit of Passion: Entrepreneurship enables you to pursue your passion and turn your interests into a fulfilling career. Whether you're passionate about a particular industry, hobby, or cause, starting your own company allows you to align your work with your personal values and goals.

3. Unlimited Potential: Unlike traditional employment, where your income may be limited by salary caps or corporate structures, starting your own company offers unlimited earning potential. As the owner, you have the opportunity to build a successful business and reap the financial rewards of your hard work and dedication.

4. Creative Freedom: Entrepreneurship provides a platform for creative expression and innovation. Whether you're launching a new product, designing a marketing campaign, or solving a problem for your customers, starting your own company allows you to unleash your creativity and bring your ideas to life.

5. Flexibility and Work-Life Balance: Running your own company offers greater flexibility and control over your work schedule. While entrepreneurship often requires long hours and hard work, it also allows you to prioritize personal commitments, family time, and leisure activities according to your preferences.

6. Personal Growth and Development: Starting a company is a journey of self-discovery and personal growth. Entrepreneurship challenges you to step outside your comfort zone, acquire new skills, and overcome obstacles, leading to greater resilience, confidence, and adaptability.

7. Making a Difference: Many entrepreneurs are driven by a desire to make a positive impact on the world. Whether through innovative products and services, job creation, or social initiatives, starting your own company allows you to contribute to positive change and leave a lasting legacy.

8. Building Wealth and Equity: As the owner of a successful company, you have the opportunity to build wealth and accumulate assets over time. In addition to earning profits from your business operations, you may also benefit from the appreciation of your company's value and the potential for future investment opportunities.

Starting your own company can be a rewarding and fulfilling journey that offers a combination of financial, professional, and personal benefits. While entrepreneurship comes with its own set of challenges and uncertainties, the opportunity to pursue your passions, achieve independence, and create something meaningful often outweighs the risks involved.

MARKET RESEARCH AND ANALYSIS

Market research and analysis are crucial steps in the process of starting and running a successful company. By gaining insights into your target market, competition, and industry trends, you can make informed decisions and develop strategies to effectively position your business for success.

Understanding your target audience is essential for identifying their needs, preferences, and behaviors. Conducting demographic research, such as age, gender, income level, and geographic location, can help you define your ideal customer profile and tailor your products or services to meet their specific needs.

Psychographic research delves deeper into the psychological and emotional factors that influence consumer behavior, such as values, attitudes, lifestyles, and purchasing motivations. By understanding what drives your target audience's purchasing decisions, you can create marketing messages and campaigns that resonate with them on a deeper level.

Analyzing your competitors is another critical aspect of market research. By assessing their strengths, weaknesses, strategies, and market share, you can identify opportunities for differentiation and competitive advantage. Conducting a competitive analysis can help you identify gaps in the market, uncover unmet needs, and position your business uniquely in the marketplace.

Moreover, staying abreast of industry trends and market dynamics is essential for anticipating changes and adapting your business strategy accordingly. Whether it's emerging technologies, shifting consumer preferences, or regulatory developments, understanding the broader market landscape can help you identify opportunities and mitigate risks.

Market research and analysis are ongoing processes that require continuous monitoring and evaluation. Regularly gathering feedback from customers, analyzing sales data, and tracking market trends can provide valuable insights that inform strategic decision-making and drive business growth.

Ultimately, market research and analysis play a critical role in helping you understand your target market, identify opportunities, and make informed decisions that enable your company to thrive in a competitive marketplace. By investing time and resources into these activities, you can position your business for long-term success and sustainable growth.

Identifying Your Target Audience

Identifying your target audience is a fundamental aspect of building a successful business. By understanding the demographics, psychographics, and behaviors of your ideal customers, you can tailor your products, services, and marketing efforts to effectively meet their needs and preferences.

Demographic factors such as age, gender, income level, education, occupation, and geographic location provide valuable insights into the characteristics of your target audience. For example, if you're selling luxury skincare products, your target audience may skew towards affluent individuals in urban areas with disposable income to spend on high-end beauty products.

Psychographic factors delve deeper into the psychological and emotional aspects of consumer behavior, including values, attitudes, lifestyles, and purchasing motivations. Understanding your target audience's psychographics can help you identify their interests, aspirations, and pain points, allowing you to create messaging and branding that resonates with them on a deeper level. For instance, if you're marketing eco-friendly household products, your target audience may prioritize sustainability and environmental consciousness in their purchasing decisions.

Behavioral factors refer to how your target audience interacts with your products or services, including their buying patterns, usage habits, brand loyalty, and purchase triggers. Analyzing consumer behavior can help you identify opportunities to enhance the customer experience, tailor your offerings to meet specific needs, and develop targeted marketing campaigns that drive engagement and conversion. For instance, if you're launching a subscription-based meal kit service, your target audience may value convenience, variety, and healthy eating options.

In addition to demographic, psychographic, and behavioral factors, it's essential to consider the size and accessibility of your target market. Conducting market research, surveys, focus groups, and competitor analysis can help you gather valuable insights and validate your assumptions about your target audience.

Identifying your target audience is a dynamic and iterative process that requires ongoing research, analysis, and refinement. By gaining a deep understanding of who your customers are, what they want, and how they behave, you can position your business for success and build meaningful relationships that drive long-term growth and profitability.

Analyzing Competitors

Analyzing competitors is a crucial component of market research that provides valuable insights into the strengths, weaknesses, strategies, and market positioning of other businesses operating in your industry. By understanding your competitors, you can identify opportunities for differentiation, benchmark your performance, and develop strategies to gain a competitive advantage.

One approach to analyzing competitors is to conduct a comprehensive competitive analysis, which involves gathering information on key competitors in your market and evaluating their performance across various dimensions. This may include:

1. Identifying Competitors: Start by identifying direct and indirect competitors that offer similar products or services to your target audience. Look for businesses that operate in the same geographic area and target the same customer segments.

2. Analyzing Products or Services: Evaluate the products or services offered by your competitors, including their features, pricing, quality, and value proposition. Compare their offerings to yours to identify areas where you can differentiate and add value to your customers.

3. Assessing Market Positioning: Examine how your competitors position themselves in the market and differentiate their brand from others. Consider factors such as brand identity, messaging, positioning, and unique selling propositions (USPs) to understand their competitive advantage.

4. Understanding Marketing and Sales Strategies: Analyze your competitors' marketing and sales strategies, including their advertising campaigns, promotional tactics, distribution channels, and customer acquisition methods. Identify which channels and tactics are most effective for reaching and engaging their target audience.

5. Evaluating Customer Experience: Assess the customer experience provided by your competitors, including factors such as customer service, user experience, and satisfaction levels. Look for opportunities to improve upon their weaknesses and provide a superior experience to your own customers.

6. Examining Financial Performance: Review your competitors' financial performance, including revenue, profit margins, market share, and growth trajectory. This can help you gauge their overall health and competitiveness within the market.

7. Monitoring Industry Trends and Developments: Stay informed about industry trends, emerging technologies, regulatory changes, and other external factors that may impact your competitors' businesses. This can help you anticipate shifts in the market landscape and adapt your strategy accordingly.

Conducting a thorough analysis of your competitors, you can gain valuable insights into their strengths and weaknesses, identify gaps in the market, and develop strategies to differentiate your business and outperform the competition. Keep in mind that competitive analysis is an ongoing process that requires regular monitoring and adjustment to stay ahead in a dynamic and competitive marketplace.

Assessing Market Trends and Demands

Assessing market trends and demands is essential for staying competitive and responsive to changing consumer preferences, technological advancements, and industry dynamics. By understanding market trends, you can identify opportunities for innovation, anticipate shifts in demand, and align your business strategies with emerging opportunities.

Here are key steps for assessing market trends and demands:

1. Industry Research: Conduct thorough research to understand the broader industry landscape, including market size, growth projections, and major players. Identify key drivers shaping the industry, such as technological advancements, regulatory changes, and consumer trends.

2. Consumer Behavior Analysis: Analyze consumer behavior patterns and preferences to identify emerging trends and demands. This may involve studying purchasing habits, lifestyle choices, demographic shifts, and psychographic factors that influence consumer decision-making.

3. Market Segmentation: Segment the market into distinct groups based on demographics, psychographics, behavior, and needs. By understanding the unique preferences and requirements of different market segments, you can tailor your products, services, and marketing strategies to better meet their needs.

4. Competitive Analysis: Assess your competitors' offerings, market positioning, and strategies to identify gaps, opportunities, and threats. Monitor competitors' product launches, marketing campaigns, pricing strategies, and customer feedback to stay informed about market dynamics and trends.

5. Technological Advancements: Stay abreast of technological advancements and innovations that may disrupt or reshape your industry. Explore emerging technologies, such as artificial intelligence, augmented reality, and block-chain, and assess their potential impact on consumer behavior and market demand.

6. Consumer Insights: Gather feedback from customers through surveys, focus groups, interviews, and social media listening to gain insights into their preferences, pain points, and unmet needs. Use qualitative and quantitative data to inform product development, marketing strategies, and customer experience enhancements.

7. Economic Indicators: Monitor economic indicators, such as GDP growth, employment rates, inflation, and consumer spending, to gauge the overall health of the economy and its impact on market demand. Economic trends can influence consumer confidence, purchasing power, and discretionary spending patterns.

8. Environmental and Social Trends: Consider environmental and social trends, such as sustainability, ethical consumption, and corporate social responsibility, which are increasingly influencing consumer behavior and market demand. Aligning your business practices with these trends can enhance your brand reputation and appeal to socially conscious consumers.

Regularly assessing market trends and demands, you can stay ahead of the curve, identify opportunities for growth, and position your business for long-term success in a dynamic and competitive marketplace. Adaptability, agility, and a customer-centric approach are key to thriving in an ever-evolving business environment.

CREATING A BUSINESS PLAN

Creating a business plan is a foundational step in launching and growing a successful business. It serves as a roadmap that outlines your business goals, strategies, and operational details, helping you clarify your vision, attract investors, and guide decision-making.

Here's how to create a comprehensive business plan:

Start with an Executive Summary: Begin your business plan with a concise executive summary that provides an overview of your business concept, target market, unique value proposition, and financial projections. This section should capture the essence of your business and entice readers to delve deeper into the plan.

Define Your Business Model: Clearly define your business model, including your products or services, target market, pricing strategy, revenue streams, and distribution channels. Explain how your business will create value for customers and generate revenue to sustain operations and drive profitability.

Conduct Market Research: Conduct thorough market research to understand your industry, target market, competitors, and market trends. Identify your target customers, their needs, preferences, and purchasing behavior, and assess the competitive landscape to identify opportunities and challenges.

Develop a Marketing and Sales Strategy: Outline your marketing and sales strategies for attracting and retaining customers. Define your brand positioning, messaging, and promotional tactics, and describe how you will reach your target audience through advertising, digital marketing, social media, and other channels.

Detail Your Operations Plan: Describe the operational aspects of your business, including your organizational structure, personnel, facilities, equipment, and suppliers. Outline your production processes, inventory management, quality control measures, and any legal or regulatory requirements that affect your operations.

Create a Financial Plan: Develop a comprehensive financial plan that includes your startup costs, revenue projections, expenses, and cash flow forecasts. Calculate your break-even point and determine your funding requirements, whether through self-funding, loans, or investment from external sources.

Include Risk Management Strategies: Identify potential risks and challenges that may impact your business and outline strategies for mitigating or addressing them. This may include market risks, competitive threats, regulatory compliance issues, supply chain disruptions, and economic downturns.

Set Milestones and Goals: Establish measurable goals and milestones to track your progress and evaluate the success of your business. Define short-term and long-term objectives for revenue growth, market penetration, customer acquisition, product development, and other key performance indicators.

Review and Revise Regularly: Regularly review and revise your business plan to reflect changes in the market, your business environment, and your strategic priorities. Update your financial projections, marketing strategies, and operational plans as needed to ensure alignment with your business goals and objectives.

Defining Your Company's Vision and Mission

Your company's vision and mission serve as guiding principles that define its purpose, values, and long-term aspirations. They provide clarity and direction, aligning stakeholders around a common vision and motivating employees to work towards shared goals.

Here's how to define your company's vision and mission:

Vision:

Your company's vision is a statement that articulates its ultimate goal or desired future state. It paints a picture of what success looks like and inspires stakeholders to rally behind a shared vision. Your vision should be ambitious, aspirational, and forward-thinking, capturing the essence of what your company aims to achieve in the long term. It should reflect your core values, beliefs, and aspirations, guiding decision-making and strategic planning.

Mission:

Your company's mission is a statement that defines its purpose, reason for existence, and how it seeks to create value for its stakeholders. It answers the question, "Why does our company exist?" and communicates the fundamental reason behind your business activities. Your mission should be clear, concise, and actionable, outlining what your company does, who it serves, and how it delivers value to customers, employees, and other stakeholders. It serves as a guiding compass that informs day-to-day operations, strategic decisions, and organizational culture.

Crafting a compelling vision and mission statement requires thoughtful consideration and reflection on your company's values, goals, and aspirations. It should capture the essence of what makes your company unique, differentiate it from competitors, and resonate with stakeholders on an emotional level. By defining your company's vision and mission, you provide a clear sense of purpose and direction that guides decision-making, inspires action, and fosters a sense of belonging and unity among employees and stakeholders.

Setting Objectives and Goals

Setting objectives and goals is a critical step in defining the direction and priorities of your business. Objectives are broad, overarching statements that outline what you want to achieve, while goals are specific, measurable targets that help you track progress towards your objectives. Here's how to set objectives and goals effectively:

Objectives:

1. Start by defining your business objectives, which represent your overarching aims and aspirations. These should align with your company's vision and mission, reflecting its long-term goals and aspirations.

2. Ensure that your objectives are specific, measurable, achievable, relevant, and time-bound (SMART). This will make them more actionable and provide a clear framework for tracking progress.

3. Consider different aspects of your business, such as financial performance, market share, customer satisfaction, employee engagement, and innovation, when setting objectives. This will help ensure a balanced approach that addresses key areas of focus.

4. Prioritize your objectives based on their importance and relevance to your business strategy. Focus on those that have the greatest impact on achieving your overall vision and mission.

5. Communicate your objectives clearly to all stakeholders, including employees, investors, customers, and partners. Ensure that everyone understands the purpose behind each objective and their role in contributing to its achievement.

Goals:

1. Once you have defined your objectives, break them down into specific, measurable goals that align with each objective. These should be concrete targets that provide a clear roadmap for achieving your objectives.

2. Make sure your goals are specific and quantifiable, with clearly defined success criteria and timelines for completion. This will enable you to track progress and measure success effectively.

3. Set realistic and achievable goals that stretch your capabilities but are within reach with effort and commitment. Avoid setting goals that are too ambitious or unrealistic, as they may lead to frustration and demotivation.

4. Break down larger goals into smaller, manageable milestones or tasks that can be accomplished incrementally. This will make it easier to track progress, stay focused, and celebrate achievements along the way.

5. Regularly review and adjust your goals as needed based on changes in the business environment, market conditions, and internal capabilities. Be flexible and adaptable, and be willing to revise your goals as circumstances evolve.

Regularly monitoring progress towards your goals and adjusting your strategy as needed will help keep your business on track and ensure that you stay aligned with your overarching vision and mission.

Developing a Revenue Model

Developing a revenue model is a fundamental aspect of building a sustainable and profitable business. It involves identifying how your company will generate revenue from the products or services you offer and determining the pricing, distribution, and sales channels that will maximize your earnings. Here's how to develop a revenue model for your business:

Start by Understanding Your Value Proposition: Before you can determine how to generate revenue, you need to understand the value you provide to your customers. Clarify the problem you solve, the benefits you offer, and why customers should choose your product or service over alternatives.

Identify Revenue Streams: Consider the various ways your business can generate revenue, such as selling products, offering services, licensing intellectual property, or monetizing data. Identify multiple revenue streams that align with your value proposition and target market.

Define Your Pricing Strategy: Determine how you will price your products or services to maximize revenue while remaining competitive in the market. Consider factors such as production costs, competitor pricing, perceived value, and customer willingness to pay. Explore different pricing models, such as cost-plus pricing, value-based pricing, subscription pricing, or freemium models, to find the approach that works best for your business.

Choose Distribution Channels: Decide how you will distribute your products or services to customers. Consider whether you will sell directly to consumers through your website, retail stores, or sales representatives, or through intermediaries such as distributors, wholesalers, or online marketplaces. Evaluate the pros and cons of each distribution channel and choose the ones that offer the best reach and efficiency for your business.

Optimize Sales Processes: Develop sales processes and strategies to effectively convert leads into paying customers. Invest in sales and marketing efforts to attract and retain customers, build brand awareness, and drive sales. Consider implementing customer relationship management (CRM) systems and sales automation tools to streamline processes and improve efficiency.

Explore Ancillary Revenue Opportunities: Look for additional ways to generate revenue beyond your core products or services. This could include offering complementary products or add-on services, upselling or cross-selling to existing customers, or monetizing customer data or insights. Explore partnerships, collaborations, or affiliate programs that can help you expand your revenue streams and reach new markets.

Monitor and Iterate: Continuously monitor your revenue model and performance metrics to identify areas for improvement and optimization. Track key performance indicators (KPIs) such as revenue growth, customer acquisition cost, customer lifetime value, and profit margins to gauge the effectiveness of your revenue model and make adjustments as needed.

Developing a comprehensive revenue model, will help you to create a sustainable and profitable business that delivers value to customers while generating revenue to support growth and innovation. Tailor your revenue model to align with your business goals, target market, and competitive landscape, and be prepared to adapt and iterate as market conditions evolve.

Crafting a Marketing and Sales Strategy

Crafting a marketing and sales strategy is essential for attracting customers, driving sales, and growing your business. It involves identifying your target audience, developing messaging and branding, and implementing tactics to effectively reach and engage potential customers.

Here's how to craft a comprehensive marketing and sales strategy:

Understand Your Target Audience: Start by defining your target audience and understanding their needs, preferences, and pain points. Conduct market research to gather insights into demographics, psychographics, and behavior, and use this information to tailor your marketing and sales efforts to resonate with your target customers.

Develop Your Value Proposition: Clarify the unique value your product or service offers to customers and articulate it in a compelling value proposition. Highlight the benefits, features, and advantages of your offering, and communicate how it solves customers' problems or fulfills their needs better than alternatives.

Create a Brand Identity: Develop a strong brand identity that reflects your company's values, personality, and positioning in the market. Design a distinctive logo, color palette, and visual elements that convey your brand's identity and resonate with your target audience. Consistently apply your brand across all marketing and sales materials to build brand recognition and loyalty.

Choose Marketing Channels: Identify the most effective marketing channels for reaching your target audience and driving engagement. Consider a mix of digital and traditional channels, such as social media, email marketing, content marketing, search engine optimization (SEO), pay-per-click (PPC) advertising, print ads, events, and networking. Tailor your marketing tactics to each channel's strengths and your audience's preferences.

Create Compelling Content: Develop high-quality content that educates, entertains, and engages your target audience. Create blog posts, articles, videos, infographics, and other content that addresses customer pain points, provides valuable information, and showcases your expertise. Share your content across various channels to attract attention and drive traffic to your website or storefront.

Implement Sales Strategies: Develop sales strategies and tactics to convert leads into customers and drive revenue. Define your sales process, from lead generation and qualification to closing deals and nurturing customer relationships. Train your sales team on effective selling techniques, objection handling, and customer relationship management to maximize sales effectiveness.

Leverage Data and Analytics: Use data and analytics to measure the performance of your marketing and sales efforts and make data-driven decisions. Track key performance indicators (KPIs) such as website traffic, conversion rates, customer acquisition cost, and customer lifetime value to assess the effectiveness of your strategies and optimize for better results.

Continuously Improve and Iterate: Regularly review and analyze your marketing and sales performance to identify areas for improvement and optimization. Test different strategies, messaging, and tactics to see what resonates best with your audience and drives the highest ROI. Stay agile and adaptable, and be willing to adjust your strategy based on changing market conditions and customer feedback.

Crafting a comprehensive marketing and sales strategy, you can attract customers, drive sales, and grow your business effectively. Tailor your strategy to your target audience, industry, and business goals, and be prepared to iterate and refine your approach over time to stay competitive and achieve sustainable growth.

LEGAL CONSIDERATIONS AND BUSINESS STRUCTURE

Legal considerations and choosing the right business structure are critical steps in starting and operating a business. These aspects ensure compliance with laws and regulations, protect personal assets, and define the operational framework of your business.

Here's what to consider:

Understand Legal Requirements: Familiarize yourself with the legal requirements and regulations that apply to your industry and location. This may include business licenses, permits, zoning laws, tax obligations, employment regulations, and intellectual property protection.

Choose the Right Business Structure: Selecting the appropriate business structure is essential for legal, financial, and operational reasons. Common options include sole proprietorship, partnership, limited liability company (LLC), corporation (C-corp or S-corp), and nonprofit organization. Consider factors such as liability protection, taxation, management flexibility, and administrative requirements when choosing a structure.

Protect Personal Assets: One of the primary benefits of choosing a legal business structure, such as an LLC or corporation, is the protection of personal assets from business liabilities. By separating your personal and business finances, you can shield personal assets, such as your home or savings, from potential lawsuits or debts incurred by the business.

Draft Contracts and Agreements: Contracts and agreements are essential for outlining the terms and conditions of business relationships with customers, vendors, employees, and partners. Work with legal professionals to draft contracts that clearly define rights, responsibilities, payment terms, confidentiality provisions, and dispute resolution mechanisms to protect your interests and minimize legal risks.

Secure Intellectual Property Rights: Protect your intellectual property (IP) assets, such as trademarks, copyrights, patents, and trade secrets, to safeguard your brand, inventions, and creative works from unauthorized use or infringement. Register trademarks and copyrights with the appropriate government agencies and implement confidentiality agreements to protect trade secrets.

Comply with Employment Laws: Understand and comply with federal, state, and local employment laws and regulations governing wages, hours, workplace safety, discrimination, harassment, and employee benefits. Develop employee policies and procedures that adhere to legal requirements and promote a safe, fair, and inclusive work environment.

Maintain Corporate Compliance: Stay compliant with ongoing legal and regulatory obligations, such as annual filings, tax returns, corporate governance requirements, and reporting obligations. Keep accurate records of corporate meetings, resolutions, and financial transactions to demonstrate compliance and maintain good standing with regulatory authorities.

Seek Legal Advice: Consult with experienced legal professionals, such as attorneys and business advisors, to navigate legal considerations and ensure compliance with applicable laws and regulations. Legal experts can provide guidance on business structuring, contract drafting, IP protection, regulatory compliance, and risk management tailored to your specific needs and circumstances.

Addressing legal considerations and choosing the right business structure, you can establish a solid legal foundation for your business, minimize legal risks, and position your company for long-term success and growth. Prioritize compliance with laws and regulations, seek professional advice when needed, and proactively address legal issues to protect your business and mitigate potential liabilities.

Choosing a Business Structure (e.g., Sole Proprietorship, LLC, Corporation)

Choosing the right business structure is a crucial decision that impacts your legal liability, tax obligations, management flexibility, and operational framework.

Here are key considerations for common business structures:

Sole Proprietorship

A sole proprietorship is the simplest and most common form of business structure, where one individual owns and operates the business. It requires no formal registration and offers complete control over business decisions. However, sole proprietors are personally liable for business debts and legal obligations, which means personal assets are at risk.

Partnership

A partnership is a business structure where two or more individuals share ownership and management responsibilities. Partnerships can be general partnerships, where all partners share equally in profits and liabilities, or limited partnerships, where one or more partners have limited liability. Partnerships offer flexibility in management and taxation but may face challenges related to decision-making and liability.

Limited Liability Company (LLC)

An LLC is a hybrid business structure that combines the limited liability protection of a corporation with the flexibility and tax advantages of a partnership. LLC owners, known as members, are not personally liable for the debts and liabilities of the business, and profits are taxed at the individual level. LLCs offer flexibility in management structure and are relatively easy to set up and maintain.

Corporation

A corporation is a separate legal entity that is owned by shareholders and managed by a board of directors. Corporations offer the highest level of personal liability protection, as shareholders' personal assets are generally shielded from business debts and liabilities. Corporations have complex legal and regulatory requirements, including formal registration, corporate governance, and compliance with tax laws. They also face double taxation, where profits are taxed at both the corporate and individual levels.

Each business structure has its own advantages and disadvantages, so it's important to carefully consider your specific needs, goals, and circumstances before choosing a structure. Factors to consider include liability protection, taxation, management flexibility, administrative requirements, and cost of formation and maintenance. Consult with legal and financial advisors to evaluate your options and determine the best business structure for your business.

Registering Your Business and Obtaining Necessary Permits

Registering your business and obtaining necessary permits are vital steps to ensure legal compliance and establish your business as a legitimate entity in the eyes of the law and your customers.

Firstly, when registering your business, you need to select a suitable name that reflects your brand identity and is unique within your industry. After deciding on a name, you must determine the legal structure of your business, such as a sole proprietorship, partnership, LLC, or corporation. Once decided, you'll need to register your business with the appropriate state government agency, typically the

Secretary of State's office. This official registration process establishes your business entity and may involve submitting required forms and paying registration fees.

Additionally, obtaining an Employer Identification Number (EIN) from the Internal Revenue Service (IRS) is essential if your business has employees, operates as a corporation or partnership, or meets other criteria. The EIN serves as a unique identifier for your business entity and is necessary for tax purposes.

Moving on to permits and licenses, it's crucial to research and understand the specific requirements applicable to your business, including general business licenses, professional licenses, health permits, zoning permits, and environmental permits. This research involves contacting local city or county government offices and relevant regulatory agencies to inquire about permit requirements, application procedures, inspections, fees, and renewal processes.

Once you've gathered necessary information, you'll need to prepare and submit permit applications, ensuring compliance with all requirements and providing supporting documentation, such as business plans, floor plans, health and safety certifications, and insurance policies. Be prepared to address any requests for additional information or modifications as needed.

Upon approval of your permit applications, it's essential to display any required permits, licenses, or certifications prominently at your business premises where they are easily visible to customers and authorities. Keeping copies of all permits and licenses on file for record-keeping purposes is also advisable.

Completing these steps, allows you demonstrate legal compliance, protect your business from potential liabilities, and build trust with customers and stakeholders. Regularly review and stay informed about ongoing regulatory obligations to ensure continued compliance and smooth operation of your business.

Understanding Copyright and Intellectual Property Laws

Understanding copyright and intellectual property laws is crucial for protecting your creative works, inventions, and business assets from unauthorized use or infringement.

Here's what you need to know:

Copyright Law

Copyright law protects original works of authorship, such as literary, artistic, musical, and dramatic works, from unauthorized reproduction, distribution, display, or performance. Copyright protection arises automatically upon the creation of a work in a tangible form, such as writing, recording, or drawing, and generally lasts for the life of the author plus 70 years.

Copyright gives the creator exclusive rights to reproduce, distribute, perform, display, and create derivative works based on their original work. These rights can be licensed or transferred to others through contracts or agreements.

Common examples of copyrighted works include books, articles, music, paintings, photographs, films, software, and website content.

Fair use is a doctrine in copyright law that allows limited use of copyrighted material without permission for purposes such as criticism, commentary, news reporting, teaching, scholarship, or research. However, fair use is determined on a case-by-case basis and depends on factors such as the purpose and character of the use, the nature of the copyrighted work, the amount and substantiality of the portion used, and the effect on the potential market for the copyrighted work.

Intellectual Property Law

Intellectual property (IP) law encompasses various legal protections for intangible assets, including patents, trademarks, copyrights, and trade secrets.

Patents protect inventions and innovations by granting the inventor exclusive rights to make, use, and sell the patented invention for a limited period, typically 20 years from the date of filing. Patents are granted for novel, useful, and non-obvious inventions in fields such as technology, science, and engineering.

Trademarks protect brand names, logos, symbols, and slogans used in commerce to identify and distinguish goods and services from those of others. Trademark registration provides exclusive rights to use the mark in connection with specific goods or services and prevents others from using confusingly similar marks.

Trade secrets are confidential and proprietary information that provides a competitive advantage to a business. Trade secrets can include formulas, processes, methods, designs, or customer lists that are not generally known or readily ascertainable by others. To maintain trade secret protection, businesses must take reasonable steps to keep the information secret, such as implementing confidentiality agreements and security measures.

Enforcement and Remedies

Enforcement of copyright and intellectual property rights involves taking legal action against individuals or entities that infringe on those rights. Remedies for infringement may include injunctions to stop the unauthorized use, monetary damages to compensate for losses, and attorney's fees and costs.

Businesses and individuals can protect their creative works, inventions, and proprietary information by registering copyrights, patents, trademarks, and trade secrets with the appropriate government agencies. Additionally, businesses can use contracts, such as non-disclosure agreements (NDAs) and licensing agreements, to establish rights and obligations related to intellectual property.

Understanding copyright and intellectual property laws is essential for safeguarding your creative and innovative endeavors, protecting your business assets, and avoiding legal disputes. Consulting with legal professionals specializing in intellectual property law can help ensure compliance and provide guidance on protecting and enforcing your intellectual property rights.

Drafting Contracts and Agreements

Drafting contracts and agreements is a critical aspect of business operations, as they establish legal obligations and protect the interests of parties involved.

Here's what you need to consider when drafting contracts and agreements:

1. Identify Parties: Clearly identify the parties entering into the contract, including their legal names, addresses, and contact information. Ensure accuracy to avoid ambiguity or confusion regarding the parties' identities.

2. Define Terms and Conditions: Clearly define the terms and conditions of the agreement, including the rights, responsibilities, and obligations of each party. Specify the scope of work, deliverables, timelines, payment terms, and any performance metrics or quality standards.

3. Outline Consideration: Clearly outline the consideration exchanged between the parties, such as monetary payments, goods, services, or other valuable assets. Specify the amount, timing, and method of payment, as well as any penalties or late fees for non-payment.

4. Include Legal Clauses: Include essential legal clauses to protect the interests of both parties and address potential risks or disputes. Common clauses include:

- **Indemnification:** Specify each party's responsibility to indemnify and hold harmless the other party from losses, damages, or liabilities arising from breaches of the agreement.

- **Limitation of Liability:** Limit the liability of each party to a certain extent, such as the amount paid under the contract or a specified cap on damages.

- **Governing Law and Jurisdiction:** Specify the governing law and jurisdiction that will govern the interpretation and enforcement of the contract in case of disputes.

- **Confidentiality:** Include provisions to protect confidential information exchanged between the parties and prohibit unauthorized disclosure or use of such information.

- **Termination:** Outline the circumstances under which either party can terminate the agreement, including notice periods and any termination fees or penalties.

5. Customize for Specific Needs: Tailor the contract language and provisions to address the specific needs and circumstances of the parties involved. Consider industry-specific requirements, unique business practices, and any special considerations or contingencies that may apply.

6. Seek Legal Review: Consider seeking legal review and advice from qualified attorneys specializing in contract law to ensure that the contract is legally enforceable, adequately protects your interests, and complies with relevant laws and regulations.

7. Execute and Maintain Records: Once the contract is finalized, ensure that all parties sign and execute the agreement according to the specified procedures. Maintain accurate records of executed contracts and related correspondence for future reference and compliance purposes.

Following these guidelines and best practices, you can draft effective contracts and agreements that establish clear expectations, mitigate risks, and protect the interests of all parties involved. Effective contract drafting requires attention to detail, clarity of language, and consideration of legal implications, so take the time to ensure that your contracts accurately reflect the intentions and agreements of the parties involved.

FINANCIAL MANAGEMENT

Financial management is essential for the success and sustainability of any business. It involves effectively managing financial resources, making strategic decisions, and implementing sound practices to achieve financial goals.

Here are key aspects of financial management:

Budgeting: Develop and maintain a budget that outlines your anticipated revenues, expenses, and cash flows for a specific period, such as a month, quarter, or year. Budgeting helps you allocate resources efficiently, identify potential areas for cost savings, and plan for future growth and investments.

Cash Flow Management: Monitor and manage cash flow to ensure that your business has enough liquidity to meet its financial obligations, such as paying bills, salaries, and suppliers, while maintaining adequate reserves for unexpected expenses or opportunities. Implement strategies to optimize cash flow, such as invoicing promptly, minimizing late payments, and managing inventory levels.

Financial Reporting: Generate accurate and timely financial reports, such as income statements, balance sheets, and cash flow statements, to track your business's financial performance and make informed decisions. Analyze key financial ratios and metrics to assess profitability, liquidity, solvency, and efficiency, and identify areas for improvement.

Profitability Analysis: Analyze your business's profitability by evaluating revenues, expenses, and margins across different products, services, customers, or geographic regions. Identify your most profitable revenue streams and focus on maximizing returns while minimizing costs and inefficiencies.

Cost Control: Implement cost control measures to manage expenses and improve profitability. Identify areas of excessive spending or waste and take steps to reduce costs through negotiation, optimization, or elimination of non-essential expenses. Regularly review and benchmark costs against industry standards and competitors to identify opportunities for cost savings.

Financial Planning and Forecasting: Develop financial plans and forecasts to guide your business's growth and investment decisions. Forecast revenues, expenses, and cash flows based on historical data, market trends, and future projections to anticipate potential challenges, opportunities, and resource needs. Adjust plans as needed to adapt to changing market conditions and business objectives.

Capital Management: Manage your business's capital structure, including debt and equity financing, to optimize financial leverage and minimize costs. Evaluate various financing options, such as loans, lines of credit, equity investments, or crowdfunding, and choose the most appropriate sources of capital based on your business's needs and risk tolerance.

Risk Management: Identify, assess, and mitigate financial risks that could impact your business's operations, profitability, or reputation. Implement risk management strategies, such as diversification, insurance coverage, hedging, or contingency planning, to protect against potential threats, such as market volatility, economic downturns, or regulatory changes.

Tax Planning and Compliance: Develop tax planning strategies to minimize tax liabilities and maximize tax efficiency while complying with applicable tax laws and regulations. Stay informed about tax deductions, credits, incentives, and filing requirements that apply to your business and seek professional advice from tax experts to optimize your tax position.

Estimating Startup Costs

Estimating startup costs is a critical step in launching a new business and requires careful planning and analysis. Startup costs encompass all expenses incurred before your business begins generating revenue and can vary significantly depending on the type of business, industry, and scale of operations.

Start by identifying and categorizing the various expenses associated with starting your business, including:

1. Initial Investment: This includes one-time expenses such as purchasing equipment, machinery, furniture, fixtures, or vehicles needed to start your business. Consider both essential and optional items required to launch your business successfully.

2. Legal and Regulatory Costs: Factor in expenses related to legal and regulatory compliance, such as business registration fees, permits, licenses, professional fees for legal or accounting services, and insurance premiums.

3. Marketing and Advertising: Budget for costs associated with marketing and advertising your business to attract customers and generate awareness. This may include expenses for branding, website development, advertising campaigns, promotional materials, and signage.

4. Technology and Software: Allocate funds for purchasing or licensing technology and software tools necessary for running your business efficiently, such as computers, software applications, point-of-sale systems, and customer relationship management (CRM) software.

5. Inventory and Supplies: Estimate the cost of purchasing initial inventory or supplies needed to produce or sell your products or services. Consider factors such as supplier costs, shipping fees, storage expenses, and inventory management systems.

6. Rent and Utilities: Account for expenses related to leasing or renting office space, retail space, or production facilities, as well as monthly utilities such as electricity, water, heating, and internet services.

7. Employee Expenses: If you plan to hire employees, budget for recruitment costs, salaries, wages, benefits, payroll taxes, and training expenses. Consider both short-term startup needs and ongoing personnel costs.

8. Contingency Fund: Set aside a contingency fund to cover unexpected expenses or emergencies that may arise during the startup phase. It's advisable to budget an additional percentage of your total estimated costs as a buffer to mitigate risks and uncertainties.

To estimate startup costs accurately, research industry benchmarks, obtain quotes from suppliers and service providers, and consult with experts or mentors familiar with your business sector. Develop a detailed budget and financial plan that outlines all anticipated expenses and sources of funding, including personal savings, loans, grants, or investments from partners or investors.

By carefully estimating startup costs and creating a realistic budget, you can better plan for financial needs, allocate resources effectively, and position your business for success as you launch and grow. Regularly review and adjust your budget as needed based on actual expenses and changing business circumstances to ensure financial sustainability and viability in the long term.

Securing Funding (if necessary)

Securing funding is often necessary to cover startup costs, operational expenses, and capital investments required to launch and grow a business.

Here are key steps to secure funding:

1. Assess Funding Needs: Determine the amount of funding needed to start and operate your business, considering startup costs, working capital requirements, and growth projections. Develop a detailed budget and financial plan to identify funding gaps and determine the type and amount of funding required.

2. Explore Funding Options: Consider various sources of funding available to entrepreneurs, including:

   - Personal Savings: Use personal savings, investments, or assets to finance your business.

   - Friends and Family: Seek financial support from friends, family members, or acquaintances who believe in your business idea.

   - Loans: Apply for small business loans from banks, credit unions, or online lenders. Explore government-backed loans or programs specifically designed for startups and small businesses.

- Investors: Pitch your business idea to angel investors, venture capitalists, or private equity firms who are willing to invest capital in exchange for equity or ownership stakes in your company.

- Crowdfunding: Launch a crowdfunding campaign on platforms such as Kickstarter, Indiegogo, or GoFundMe to raise funds from a large number of individual backers in exchange for rewards, pre-orders, or equity.

- Grants: Research and apply for grants, scholarships, or government funding programs available to startups and entrepreneurs in your industry or location.

3. Prepare a Compelling Pitch: Develop a compelling business plan and pitch deck that clearly articulates your business idea, market opportunity, competitive advantage, financial projections, and funding needs. Tailor your pitch to the specific preferences and criteria of potential investors or lenders.

4. Build Relationships: Network and build relationships with potential investors, lenders, and funding sources through industry events, networking groups, pitch competitions, and mentorship programs. Leverage your existing connections and seek introductions to key decision-makers in your target funding organizations.

5. Present Your Case: Present your business plan and pitch to potential investors or lenders in formal meetings, presentations, or pitch events. Be prepared to answer questions, address concerns, and provide additional information or documentation as requested.

6. Negotiate Terms: Negotiate terms and conditions of funding agreements, including interest rates, repayment terms, equity stakes, or other financial arrangements. Seek legal advice to review and negotiate contracts or agreements to ensure they protect your interests and align with your business goals.

7. Follow Up and Close: Follow up with potential investors or lenders after initial meetings or pitches to provide updates, answer questions, and continue discussions. Work towards finalizing funding agreements, securing commitments, and closing deals to access the capital needed to launch or grow your business.

Budgeting for Equipment, Software, and Personnel

Budgeting for equipment, software, and personnel is a critical aspect of financial planning for any business. Allocating funds for these resources ensures that your business has the necessary tools, technology, and human capital to operate efficiently and effectively.

Here's what you need to consider:

Equipment: Budgeting for equipment involves identifying and estimating the costs associated with purchasing or leasing essential physical assets needed to run your business. This may include machinery, tools, vehicles, office furniture, fixtures, or specialized equipment required for production, operations, or service delivery. Consider factors such as equipment specifications, quality, warranties, maintenance requirements, and potential financing options when budgeting for equipment expenses.

Software: Budgeting for software involves estimating the costs associated with acquiring or subscribing to necessary software applications, platforms, or tools to support various business functions and processes. This may include accounting software, customer relationship management (CRM) systems, inventory management software, productivity tools, communication platforms, or industry-specific software solutions. Consider factors such as licensing fees, subscription costs, implementation and training expenses, integration requirements, and ongoing support and maintenance when budgeting for software expenses.

Personnel: Budgeting for personnel involves estimating the costs associated with hiring, compensating, and managing employees or contractors needed to perform various roles and responsibilities within your business. This may include salaries, wages, benefits, payroll taxes, recruitment expenses, training costs, and employee-related expenses such as insurance, retirement contributions, and paid time off. Consider factors such as labor market conditions, industry benchmarks, employee retention strategies, and growth projections when budgeting for personnel expenses.

When budgeting for equipment, software, and personnel, it's essential to:

- Conduct thorough research to identify the specific equipment, software, and personnel needs of your business based on its size, industry, stage of development, and growth plans.

- Obtain quotes or estimates from multiple suppliers, vendors, or service providers to compare costs, quality, and terms before making purchasing decisions.

- Factor in additional expenses such as installation, setup, training, customization, or ongoing support when estimating total costs.

- Allocate funds for contingency or unexpected expenses that may arise during the procurement, implementation, or operation of equipment, software, or personnel.

- Regularly review and update your budget for equipment, software, and personnel to reflect changes in business needs, market conditions, or financial performance.

Prioritize investments that align with your strategic priorities, enhance productivity, and drive long-term growth and profitability.

Setting Pricing Strategies

Setting pricing strategies is a crucial aspect of business management that requires careful consideration and analysis. Your pricing strategy directly impacts your revenue, profitability, market positioning, and customer perception.

Here are key factors to consider when setting pricing strategies:

Market Analysis: Conduct thorough market research to understand your target customers, competitors, and industry dynamics. Identify pricing trends, customer preferences, and competitive pricing strategies to inform your pricing decisions.

Cost Analysis: Calculate all costs associated with producing, marketing, and selling your products or services, including materials, labor, overhead, and operating expenses. Determine your desired profit margins and establish pricing that covers your costs while generating a reasonable profit.

Value Proposition: Evaluate the unique value proposition of your products or services and how they differentiate from competitors. Consider the perceived value to customers and their willingness to pay based on factors such as quality, features, benefits, brand reputation, and customer service.

Pricing Objectives: Define your pricing objectives based on your business goals and market positioning. Common pricing objectives include maximizing revenue, capturing market share, maintaining price stability, achieving profit targets, or enhancing customer loyalty.

Competitive Analysis: Analyze the pricing strategies of your competitors to assess their pricing levels, pricing structures, discounts, promotions, and value-added services. Determine how your pricing strategy will position your business relative to competitors and appeal to target customers.

Pricing Models: Choose the most suitable pricing model or strategy for your products or services based on factors such as market demand, customer segments, product lifecycle, and competitive landscape. Common pricing models include cost-plus pricing, value-based pricing, competitive pricing, dynamic pricing, and penetration pricing.

Price Discrimination: Consider implementing price discrimination strategies to capture additional revenue by charging different prices to different customer segments based on their willingness to pay, usage patterns, or purchasing behavior. Examples of price discrimination include tiered pricing, volume discounts, loyalty programs, and promotional pricing.

Psychological Pricing: Utilize psychological pricing techniques to influence customer perceptions and behavior. Strategies such as charm pricing (ending prices with .99 or .95), prestige pricing (setting high prices to convey exclusivity or luxury), or decoy pricing (introducing a higher-priced option to make other options appear more attractive) can impact purchase decisions.

Testing and Optimization: Continuously monitor and analyze the effectiveness of your pricing strategy through testing, experimentation, and data analysis. Adjust pricing levels, structures, or promotions based on customer feedback, sales performance, and competitive dynamics to optimize revenue and profitability.

Legal and Ethical Considerations: Ensure that your pricing practices comply with applicable laws, regulations, and ethical standards. Avoid deceptive pricing tactics, price-fixing agreements, or unfair competition practices that could harm consumers or violate antitrust laws.

Regularly review and adjust your pricing strategies to adapt to changing market conditions, customer preferences, and business goals.

Equipment And Technology

Equipment and technology are essential components of modern businesses, enabling efficient operations, productivity, and innovation.

 Here's how businesses can leverage equipment and technology effectively:

1. Identify Needs: Assess your business's specific equipment and technology needs based on your industry, processes, and objectives. Determine which tools, machinery, software, and hardware are essential to support your operations and achieve your business goals.

2. Procurement: Research, evaluate, and procure the necessary equipment and technology solutions from reputable suppliers, vendors, or manufacturers. Consider factors such as quality, reliability, functionality, compatibility, and cost-effectiveness when selecting equipment and technology options.

3. Investment Considerations: Evaluate the total cost of ownership (TCO) of equipment and technology solutions, including acquisition costs, installation, maintenance, upgrades, and ongoing support. Consider financing options, such as leasing, equipment loans, or vendor financing, to manage upfront costs and preserve cash flow.

4. Integration: Integrate equipment and technology seamlessly into your business processes and workflows to maximize efficiency and productivity. Ensure compatibility with existing systems, software, and infrastructure to minimize disruptions and optimize performance.

5. Training and Support: Provide comprehensive training and support to employees to ensure they can effectively utilize and leverage the capabilities of equipment and technology solutions. Offer training programs, user manuals, tutorials, and ongoing technical assistance to enhance proficiency and address any issues or challenges.

6. Maintenance and Upkeep: Implement regular maintenance schedules and protocols to keep equipment and technology systems in optimal condition and minimize downtime. Conduct routine inspections, repairs, upgrades, and performance optimizations to prolong equipment lifespan and ensure reliability.

7. Security and Data Protection: Implement robust security measures and protocols to safeguard equipment and technology systems from cyber threats, unauthorized access, data breaches, and information theft. Use encryption, firewalls, access controls, and security software to protect sensitive data and intellectual property.

8. Scalability and Future-Proofing: Invest in scalable and flexible equipment and technology solutions that can accommodate future growth, expansion, or changes in business needs. Choose technologies that offer upgradability, interoperability, and compatibility with emerging trends and innovations.

9. Innovation and Competitive Advantage: Leverage equipment and technology to drive innovation, differentiation, and competitive advantage in your industry. Explore new technologies, automation, digital transformation initiatives, and process improvements to enhance efficiency, streamline operations, and deliver superior value to customers.

10. Continuous Improvement: Continuously evaluate and optimize your equipment and technology investments to adapt to changing business requirements, technological advancements, and market dynamics. Monitor performance metrics, solicit feedback from stakeholders, and implement improvements to drive ongoing innovation and success.

Selecting Cameras, Lenses, and Accessories

Selecting cameras, lenses, and accessories is a crucial decision for individuals or businesses involved in photography, videography, or content creation.

Here are key considerations to keep in mind:

Camera Type: Choose a camera type that best suits your needs and preferences, whether it's a DSLR (Digital Single-Lens Reflex), mirrorless, point-and-shoot, or action camera. Consider factors such as image quality, size, weight, ease of use, and compatibility with existing equipment and accessories.

Resolution and Sensor Size: Consider the resolution and sensor size of the camera, which affect image quality, detail, and low-light performance. Higher resolution and larger sensor sizes generally result in better image quality and greater flexibility in post-processing.

Lens Compatibility: Ensure compatibility between the camera body and interchangeable lenses, considering factors such as lens mount type, focal length, aperture range, and image stabilization capabilities. Invest in a versatile selection of lenses to cover a range of shooting scenarios, including wide-angle, standard, telephoto, and specialty lenses.

Lens Quality: Invest in high-quality lenses that offer sharpness, clarity, and optical performance suitable for your specific photography or videography needs. Consider factors such as lens construction, glass quality, optical coatings, and autofocus speed and accuracy when selecting lenses.

Accessories: Consider accessories such as tripods, camera bags, filters, memory cards, batteries, chargers, lens cleaning kits, and external flashes to complement your camera and enhance your shooting experience. Invest in accessories that improve convenience, protection, stability, and creativity in your photography or videography endeavors.

Budget and Value: Determine your budget and balance it with the value and features offered by different camera models, lenses, and accessories. Consider factors such as brand reputation, warranty coverage, customer support, and resale value when evaluating the overall value proposition.

User Experience: Test cameras, lenses, and accessories in person, if possible, to assess ergonomics, handling, menu navigation, and overall user experience. Consider factors such as touchscreen interfaces, customizable controls, viewfinder quality, and connectivity options when evaluating usability.

Reviews and Recommendations: Research online reviews, user feedback, and expert recommendations from reputable sources to gather insights and recommendations on specific camera models, lenses, and accessories. Consider real-world experiences and testimonials from other photographers or videographers to inform your purchasing decisions.

Future Compatibility: Consider future compatibility and upgrade paths when selecting cameras, lenses, and accessories. Choose systems and equipment that offer a wide range of compatible accessories, lenses, and upgrades to accommodate future needs, advancements, and expansions.

Ultimately, the selection of cameras, lenses, and accessories depends on your specific photography or videography requirements, preferences, and budget constraints. Take the time to research, compare options, and test equipment to ensure that your chosen gear aligns with your creative vision and enables you to capture stunning images and videos effectively.

Investing in Editing Software and Hardware

Investing in editing software and hardware is essential for individuals or businesses involved in video production, photography, graphic design, or multimedia content creation. Here are key considerations when selecting editing software and hardware:

Editing Software:

1. Features and Functionality: Choose editing software that offers a comprehensive suite of features and functionality to meet your specific needs and requirements. Look for capabilities such as video editing, audio editing, color correction, special effects, motion graphics, and integration with other software tools.

2. User Interface: Consider the user interface of the editing software, including layout, organization, and ease of use. Opt for intuitive software with a user-friendly interface that allows for efficient navigation, editing, and workflow management.

3. Compatibility: Ensure compatibility between the editing software and your operating system (e.g., Windows, MacOS) and hardware specifications (e.g., CPU, GPU, RAM). Choose software that supports the file formats, codecs, and resolutions commonly used in your industry or workflow.

4. Performance and Speed: Prioritize editing software that offers fast rendering and processing capabilities to optimize productivity and workflow efficiency. Look for software that utilizes hardware acceleration, multi-core processing, and GPU acceleration for smoother playback and real-time editing.

5. Support and Updates: Consider the level of technical support, documentation, and community resources available for the editing software. Choose software from reputable developers or companies that provide regular updates, bug fixes, tutorials, and customer support services.

Editing Hardware:

1. Computer System: Invest in a powerful computer system with sufficient processing power, memory (RAM), storage, and graphics capabilities to handle the demands of editing software and multimedia content creation. Consider factors such as CPU performance, GPU acceleration, RAM capacity, and storage type (e.g., SSD vs. HDD).

2. Graphics Card (GPU): Choose a dedicated graphics card (GPU) with sufficient VRAM and compute power to accelerate rendering, playback, and processing tasks in editing software. Look for GPUs optimized for creative applications and video editing workloads.

3. Display Monitor: Select a high-quality display monitor with accurate color reproduction, resolution, and screen size to ensure accurate color grading, image editing, and visual quality assessment. Consider factors such as panel technology (e.g., IPS, OLED), color gamut coverage (e.g., sRGB, Adobe RGB), and display calibration capabilities.

4. Input Devices: Invest in ergonomic input devices such as keyboards, mice, graphics tablets, or editing controllers to facilitate precise control, navigation, and manipulation of editing software. Choose devices with customizable buttons, shortcuts, and programmable features to streamline workflow and increase productivity.

5. Storage Solutions: Implement robust storage solutions, such as external hard drives, RAID arrays, or network-attached storage (NAS), to store and manage large multimedia files, project assets, and archives. Consider factors such as storage capacity, speed, reliability, and data redundancy to ensure data integrity and accessibility.

Investing in editing software and hardware that align with your workflow, requirements, and budget, you can enhance productivity, creativity, and quality in your multimedia content creation endeavors. Evaluate software and hardware options based on features, performance, compatibility, support, and long-term value to make informed decisions that support your creative vision and business objectives.

Building a Post-Production Setup

Building a post-production setup is a crucial step for individuals or businesses involved in video production, photography, graphic design, or multimedia content creation.

Here's how to build an effective post-production setup:

1. Define Requirements: Determine your specific post-production requirements based on the type of content you produce, your workflow, and your budget. Consider factors such as editing software, hardware specifications, storage needs, and workspace layout.

2. Select Editing Software: Choose editing software that suits your needs and preferences, whether it's video editing software (e.g., Adobe Premiere Pro, Final Cut Pro, DaVinci Resolve), photo editing software (e.g., Adobe Photoshop, Lightroom), or graphic design software (e.g., Adobe Illustrator, InDesign). Evaluate features, pricing, compatibility, and user interface to make an informed decision.

3. Invest in Hardware: Invest in high-performance hardware to support your editing software and workflow requirements. This includes a powerful computer system with a fast CPU, ample RAM, dedicated graphics card (GPU), and sufficient storage capacity (e.g., SSD for speed, HDD for storage). Consider peripherals such as monitors, input devices, and audio equipment to enhance productivity and user experience.

4. Set Up Editing Workspace: Design and set up a dedicated editing workspace that is comfortable, ergonomic, and conducive to creativity and productivity. Arrange your computer, monitors, input devices, and other equipment in an organized manner to optimize workflow efficiency. Consider factors such as lighting, acoustics, and ergonomic furniture to create an optimal working environment.

5. Establish Data Management: Implement robust data management practices to organize, store, and backup your multimedia files, project assets, and archives. Set up a centralized storage solution such as external hard drives, NAS, or cloud storage to store and access files securely. Develop a file naming convention, folder structure, and backup schedule to maintain data integrity and accessibility.

6. Customize Software Settings: Customize editing software settings, preferences, and keyboard shortcuts to streamline workflow and optimize efficiency. Configure project settings, render settings, and output settings to ensure compatibility with your desired output formats, resolutions, and delivery platforms.

7. Integrate Workflow Tools: Integrate workflow tools, plugins, and third-party applications to enhance functionality, automate repetitive tasks, and extend the capabilities of your editing software. Explore options for color grading, audio editing, visual effects, motion graphics, and collaboration tools to optimize post-production workflow.

8. Training and Skill Development: Invest in training, education, and skill development to master editing software and techniques and stay updated with industry trends and best practices. Attend workshops, online courses, tutorials, and industry events to enhance your editing skills and expand your creative capabilities.

9. Test and Iterate: Test your post-production setup, software, and workflow to identify any inefficiencies, bottlenecks, or areas for improvement. Iterate and refine your setup based on feedback, performance metrics, and user experience to optimize productivity and quality.

10. Maintain and Upgrade: Regularly maintain and update your post-production setup, software, and hardware to ensure optimal performance, reliability, and security. Stay informed about software updates, hardware advancements, and industry standards to make informed decisions about upgrades and investments.

Exploring Specialized Equipment (e.g., Drones, Stabilizers)

Exploring specialized equipment such as drones and stabilizers can significantly enhance the capabilities and quality of your video production or photography projects.

Here's how you can explore and integrate specialized equipment into your workflow:

Research and Understand: Begin by researching and understanding the capabilities, features, and benefits of specialized equipment such as drones, stabilizers (e.g., gimbals), sliders, jibs, or underwater housings. Learn about their applications, limitations, and best practices for usage in various shooting scenarios.

Evaluate Needs: Evaluate your specific project requirements, creative vision, and budget constraints to determine which specialized equipment would best suit your needs. Consider factors such as the type of shots you want to achieve, environmental conditions, and logistical considerations when selecting equipment.

Demo and Test: Whenever possible, demo or rent specialized equipment to test its performance, usability, and compatibility with your existing gear. Experiment with different settings, techniques, and shooting scenarios to assess how the equipment enhances your creative capabilities and workflow.

Training and Skill Development: Invest in training, education, and skill development to learn how to operate specialized equipment effectively and achieve professional-quality results. Take advantage of tutorials, workshops, online courses, and user manuals to master techniques and best practices for using the equipment.

Integration with Workflow: Integrate specialized equipment seamlessly into your production workflow to maximize efficiency and creativity. Ensure compatibility with your existing camera gear, editing software, and post-production processes. Develop standardized procedures and protocols for using specialized equipment to streamline operations and ensure consistency.

Safety and Compliance: Prioritize safety and compliance when using specialized equipment such as drones, particularly when operating in public spaces or sensitive environments. Familiarize yourself with local regulations, airspace restrictions, and safety guidelines governing the use of drones and other specialized equipment.

Creative Exploration: Experiment with creative techniques and shot compositions enabled by specialized equipment to push the boundaries of your storytelling and visual aesthetics. Explore unique perspectives, angles, movements, and effects that add depth, dynamism, and immersion to your projects.

Collaboration and Networking: Collaborate with other professionals, creatives, and enthusiasts who specialize in using specialized equipment to share knowledge, insights, and inspiration. Attend industry events, workshops, and meetups to network with experts and enthusiasts and stay informed about the latest trends and innovations in specialized equipment.

Feedback and Iteration: Seek feedback from peers, clients, and audiences to evaluate the effectiveness of specialized equipment in achieving your project goals and satisfying stakeholder expectations. Iterate and refine your approach based on feedback, performance metrics, and lessons learned from each project.

Exploring specialized equipment and integrating it thoughtfully into your workflow, you can unlock new creative possibilities, elevate the quality of your productions, and differentiate yourself in a competitive market. Stay curious, open-minded, and adaptive to emerging technologies and techniques to continuously evolve and innovate in your craft.

BUILDING YOUR TEAM

Building your team is a critical step in establishing and growing your video production company.

Here's how to approach building a talented and cohesive team:

Identify Roles and Skills: Determine the specific roles and skill sets needed to execute your projects effectively. Consider positions such as videographers, editors, producers, directors, cinematographers, sound designers, motion graphics artists, and production assistants. Identify the technical, creative, and interpersonal skills required for each role.

Recruitment and Hiring: Recruit and hire team members who possess the skills, experience, and passion necessary to contribute to your company's success. Utilize job boards, networking events, referrals, and social media to attract qualified candidates. Conduct thorough interviews, portfolio reviews, and skills assessments to evaluate candidates' suitability for the role.

Cultural Fit: Prioritize cultural fit when selecting team members to ensure alignment with your company's values, vision, and work culture. Look for candidates who demonstrate collaboration, creativity, professionalism, and a commitment to excellence.

Consider factors such as communication style, attitude, and personality when assessing cultural fit.

Training and Development: Invest in training and development programs to onboard new team members effectively and enhance their skills and knowledge. Provide opportunities for ongoing learning, mentorship, and professional development to support career growth and retention. Foster a culture of continuous improvement and innovation within your team.

Clear Roles and Responsibilities: Define clear roles, responsibilities, and expectations for each team member to promote accountability, clarity, and alignment. Establish workflows, processes, and communication channels to facilitate collaboration, coordination, and project management. Encourage open communication, feedback, and transparency within the team.

Collaborative Environment: Foster a collaborative and supportive environment where team members feel valued, respected, and empowered to contribute their ideas and talents. Encourage creativity, experimentation, and innovation by providing a safe space for brainstorming, problem-solving, and exploring new approaches.

Effective Leadership: Provide strong leadership and direction to guide your team toward achieving common goals and objectives. Lead by example, inspire trust and confidence, and empower team members to take ownership of their work. Communicate clearly, set realistic expectations, and provide constructive feedback and recognition to motivate and inspire your team.

Diversity and Inclusion: Embrace diversity and inclusion within your team by fostering a culture of respect, equity, and belonging. Seek diversity in backgrounds, perspectives, and experiences to enrich creativity, collaboration, and decision-making. Create opportunities for all team members to contribute and thrive regardless of race, gender, age, or background.

Team Building Activities: Organize team building activities, social events, and off-site retreats to strengthen bonds, build camaraderie, and foster a sense of community within your team. Encourage collaboration, teamwork, and mutual support through shared experiences and interactions outside of work.

Recognition and Rewards: Recognize and reward team members for their contributions, achievements, and milestones. Celebrate successes, milestones, and achievements as a team to reinforce a culture of appreciation, motivation, and engagement. Offer incentives, bonuses, or perks to recognize exceptional performance and foster loyalty and commitment.

Hiring Key Personnel (e.g., Videographers, Editors, Producers)

Hiring key personnel, such as videographers, editors, and producers, is essential for establishing a successful video production company.

Here's how to approach hiring key personnel:

Identify Roles and Responsibilities: Clearly define the roles and responsibilities of key personnel based on your company's needs, projects, and objectives. Determine the specific skills, experience, and expertise required for each role, considering factors such as videography, editing, storytelling, project management, and client communication.

Recruitment Strategy: Develop a recruitment strategy to attract qualified candidates for key positions within your company. Utilize job boards, industry networks, social media platforms, and professional organizations to advertise job openings and reach potential candidates. Leverage your existing network and connections to source referrals and recommendations.

Candidate Evaluation: Review resumes, portfolios, demo reels, and work samples to evaluate candidates' qualifications, experience, and suitability for the role. Conduct interviews, phone screenings, or skills assessments to assess candidates' technical skills, creativity, problem-solving abilities, and fit with your company culture.

Cultural Fit: Prioritize cultural fit when hiring key personnel to ensure alignment with your company's values, vision, and work culture. Look for candidates who demonstrate professionalism, teamwork, creativity, and a passion for storytelling. Assess candidates' communication skills, attitude, and compatibility with your team dynamics.

Technical Expertise: Seek candidates with technical expertise and proficiency in relevant software, equipment, and tools used in video production. Look for candidates with experience using industry-standard editing software (e.g., Adobe Premiere Pro, Final Cut Pro), camera equipment, audio recording devices, and lighting setups. Evaluate candidates' technical skills through portfolio reviews, technical tests, or practical demonstrations.

Creativity and Innovation: Look for candidates who demonstrate creativity, innovation, and a strong artistic vision in their work. Seek individuals who can bring fresh ideas, perspectives, and storytelling techniques to your projects. Assess candidates' creative portfolios, projects, or concepts to evaluate their ability to produce engaging and visually compelling content.

Project Management Skills: Evaluate candidates' project management skills, organizational abilities, and attention to detail, particularly for roles such as producers or project managers. Look for candidates who can effectively manage timelines, budgets, resources, and client expectations while delivering high-quality results on schedule.

Collaborative Spirit: Look for team players who can collaborate effectively with colleagues, clients, and external partners to achieve shared goals and objectives. Seek candidates who demonstrate strong interpersonal skills, communication abilities, and a willingness to contribute to a collaborative and supportive work environment.

Long-Term Vision: Hire key personnel who share your long-term vision for the company and are committed to contributing to its growth and success. Look for individuals who are ambitious, entrepreneurial, and invested in building a thriving and sustainable video production business. Assess candidates' career goals, aspirations, and alignment with your company's values and mission.

Hiring key personnel who possess the right combination of skills, experience, creativity, and cultural fit, you can build a talented and cohesive team that drives the success and growth of your video production company. Invest time and effort in recruiting, evaluating, and onboarding key personnel to ensure that they contribute positively to your company's culture, reputation, and bottom line.

Freelancers vs. Full-time Employees

When it comes to staffing your video production company, you'll likely face the decision between hiring freelancers or full-time employees. Each option has its pros and cons, and the right choice will depend on your business needs, budget, and project requirements.

Freelancers offer flexibility and scalability, allowing you to hire talent on a project-by-project basis without the commitment of full-time employment. You can access a diverse pool of skilled professionals with specialized expertise to meet specific project needs. Freelancers often bring fresh perspectives and ideas to your projects, enhancing creativity and innovation. Additionally, hiring freelancers can be cost-effective, as you only pay for their services when needed, without the overhead of employee benefits or salaries.

However, working with freelancers may present challenges in terms of consistency, reliability, and communication. Freelancers may have multiple clients and projects competing for their time, making it challenging to secure their availability or prioritize your projects. Coordination and collaboration with freelancers may require additional effort and time to align schedules, expectations, and deliverables. Moreover, freelancers may lack a deep understanding of your company's culture, brand, and long-term vision, which can impact project cohesion and consistency.

On the other hand, hiring full-time employees offers stability, loyalty, and commitment to your company's mission and goals. Full-time employees are fully dedicated to your projects and can provide consistent support, expertise, and continuity throughout the production process. By investing in employee development and training, you can cultivate a skilled and cohesive team that shares your company's values and works collaboratively to achieve common objectives.

However, hiring full-time employees entails higher costs, including salaries, benefits, taxes, and overhead expenses. You'll need to budget for ongoing payroll expenses, regardless of project workload or revenue fluctuations. Additionally, hiring full-time employees may limit your flexibility and scalability, as you'll need to consider factors such as hiring, onboarding, and managing personnel, even during slow periods or off-seasons.

Ultimately, the decision between freelancers and full-time employees will depend on your business model, project requirements, and long-term goals. Consider factors such as project duration, complexity, budget, and resource availability when determining the most suitable staffing approach for each project. You may choose to leverage a combination of freelancers and full-time employees to strike the right balance between flexibility, scalability, consistency, and expertise, depending on your evolving business needs and project dynamics.

Cultivating a Creative and Collaborative Work Environment

Cultivating a creative and collaborative work environment is essential for fostering innovation, productivity, and employee satisfaction in your video production company.

Here's how to create an environment that encourages creativity and collaboration:

1. Encourage Open Communication: Foster a culture of open communication where team members feel comfortable sharing ideas, feedback, and concerns. Create opportunities for brainstorming sessions, team meetings, and informal discussions to facilitate dialogue and collaboration. Encourage active listening and respect for diverse perspectives to promote a culture of inclusivity and mutual respect.

2. Promote Creativity and Innovation: Provide opportunities for creative expression, experimentation, and innovation within your team. Encourage team members to think outside the box, take risks, and explore new ideas and approaches. Celebrate creativity and recognize innovative contributions to inspire a culture of continuous improvement and ingenuity.

3. Create Collaborative Spaces: Design collaborative workspaces that facilitate teamwork, interaction, and idea exchange. Consider implementing open floor plans, communal areas, and collaborative tools such as whiteboards, brainstorming walls, and project management software. Create spaces where team members can collaborate, brainstorm, and co-create in a conducive and inspiring environment.

4. Foster Cross-functional Collaboration: Encourage collaboration across different departments, disciplines, and skill sets within your company. Break down silos and foster interdisciplinary collaboration by involving team members from various backgrounds, expertise areas, and roles in project teams and initiatives. Encourage cross-training and knowledge sharing to enhance collaboration and innovation across the organization.

5. Support a Growth Mindset: Cultivate a growth mindset culture that values learning, development, and continuous improvement. Encourage team members to embrace challenges, learn from failures, and seek opportunities for growth and development. Provide access to training, workshops, and resources to support skill development, creativity, and personal growth.

6. Foster a Supportive Team Culture: Build a supportive and nurturing team culture where team members feel valued, respected, and empowered to contribute their ideas and talents. Encourage collaboration, cooperation, and mutual support among team members by fostering a sense of camaraderie, trust, and shared purpose. Celebrate achievements, milestones, and successes as a team to reinforce a positive and supportive work environment.

7. Lead by Example: Lead by example and demonstrate a commitment to creativity, collaboration, and teamwork in your own actions and behaviors. Communicate openly, listen attentively, and show appreciation for team members' contributions and efforts. Set high standards for creativity, quality, and professionalism, and inspire others to strive for excellence in their work.

8. Provide Resources and Support: Provide the necessary resources, tools, and support to enable creativity and collaboration within your team. Invest in state-of-the-art equipment, software, and technology solutions to support creative endeavors. Offer mentorship, coaching, and support to help team members overcome challenges and unleash their full creative potential.

FINDING CLIENTS AND PROJECTS

Finding clients and projects is essential for the success and growth of your video production company.

Here are strategies to help you find clients and secure projects:

Networking: Build and nurture relationships with potential clients, industry peers, and collaborators through networking events, industry conferences, and professional organizations. Attend networking events, participate in online forums and communities, and leverage social media platforms to connect with prospects and expand your professional network.

Referrals: Leverage your existing client base, colleagues, and industry contacts to generate referrals and recommendations. Encourage satisfied clients to refer you to their networks and offer incentives or rewards for referrals that lead to new projects. Cultivate positive relationships with clients and partners to encourage repeat business and referrals.

Online Presence: Establish a strong online presence through your website, social media profiles, and online portfolios to showcase your work, expertise, and capabilities. Optimize your website for search engines (SEO) to improve visibility and attract organic traffic. Share case studies, client testimonials, and project highlights to demonstrate your value and credibility to potential clients.

Marketing and Promotion: Develop a targeted marketing strategy to reach your ideal clients and promote your services effectively. Create compelling marketing materials such as brochures, business cards, and demo reels to showcase your work and highlight your unique selling points. Explore digital marketing channels such as email marketing, content marketing, and paid advertising to reach your target audience and generate leads.

Cold Outreach: Proactively reach out to potential clients through cold outreach strategies such as email campaigns, cold calls, and direct mail. Research your target market, identify potential leads, and personalize your outreach messages to demonstrate your understanding of their needs and challenges. Follow up persistently and professionally to nurture leads and convert them into clients.

Partnerships and Collaborations: Explore partnerships and collaborations with complementary businesses, agencies, or freelancers to expand your reach and access new clients and projects. Collaborate on joint projects, cross-promotional campaigns, or referral agreements to leverage each other's networks, expertise, and resources.

Industry Events and Trade Shows: Participate in industry events, trade shows, and exhibitions to showcase your work, network with potential clients, and stay informed about industry trends and opportunities. Exhibit at trade shows, sponsor industry events, or participate in panel discussions and speaking engagements to raise your profile and attract attention from potential clients.

RFPs and Bids: Monitor requests for proposals (RFPs), bid opportunities, and procurement processes in your industry or target market. Respond to RFPs with tailored proposals that demonstrate your understanding of the client's requirements, showcase your capabilities, and differentiate your offering from competitors. Develop strong relationships with procurement officers and decision-makers to increase your chances of winning bids and securing projects.

Networking within the Industry

Networking within the industry is essential for building relationships, expanding your professional network, and unlocking new opportunities in the video production industry. Here's how you can effectively network within the industry:

Attend Industry Events: Attend industry events, conferences, seminars, and trade shows related to video production, filmmaking, and media to meet and connect with industry professionals. Take advantage of networking opportunities during breaks, receptions, and social events to introduce yourself, exchange contact information, and engage in meaningful conversations.

Join Professional Organizations: Join professional organizations, associations, and societies dedicated to video production, such as the National Association of Broadcasters (NAB), the International Documentary Association (IDA), or the American Film Institute (AFI). Participate in networking events, workshops, and membership meetings to connect with peers, mentors, and industry leaders.

Utilize Online Platforms: Leverage online platforms and social media networks such as LinkedIn, Facebook, and Twitter to connect with industry professionals, join relevant groups and communities, and participate in discussions and forums. Share your work, insights, and industry updates to establish your credibility and visibility within the industry.

Attend Workshops and Masterclasses: Enroll in workshops, masterclasses, and training programs offered by industry experts, educators, and institutions to learn new skills, techniques, and trends in video production. Network with instructors, fellow participants, and guest speakers to expand your network and exchange knowledge and experiences.

Volunteer and Collaborate: Volunteer for industry-related events, film festivals, or community projects to gain exposure, build relationships, and contribute to the industry. Offer your skills, expertise, or services to collaborate with other professionals on creative projects, short films, or independent productions. Collaborate on projects with peers to showcase your talents and build your portfolio while forging valuable connections.

Attend Film Screenings and Festivals: Attend film screenings, festivals, and screenings to discover emerging talent, network with filmmakers, and stay informed about industry trends and developments. Engage with filmmakers, producers, and distributors during Q&A sessions, networking events, and after-parties to establish connections and explore potential collaborations.

Follow Up and Nurture Relationships: Follow up with contacts you meet through networking events, industry gatherings, or online platforms to maintain relationships and explore potential collaboration opportunities. Send personalized follow-up emails, connect on social media, and schedule coffee meetings or phone calls to deepen relationships and stay top-of-mind.

Be Authentic and Generous: Approach networking with authenticity, sincerity, and generosity by genuinely expressing interest in others, listening attentively, and offering support, advice, or assistance where possible. Be proactive in helping others and offering value without expecting immediate returns, as building genuine relationships takes time and effort.

UTILIZING ONLINE PLATFORMS AND SOCIAL MEDIA

Utilizing online platforms and social media is crucial for expanding your reach, building your brand, and connecting with potential clients and collaborators in the video production industry.

Here's how you can effectively leverage online platforms and social media:

Establish a Strong Online Presence: Create a professional website that showcases your portfolio, services, expertise, and contact information. Ensure that your website is user-friendly, mobile-responsive, and visually appealing to engage visitors and leave a lasting impression. Regularly update your website with new projects, testimonials, and blog posts to keep it fresh and relevant.

Utilize Social Media Channels: Create profiles on popular social media platforms such as LinkedIn, Facebook, Twitter, Instagram, and YouTube to connect with your target audience and industry peers. Customize your profiles with high-quality visuals, compelling descriptions, and relevant keywords to attract followers and enhance visibility. Post regularly on social media to share updates, behind-the-scenes content, industry insights, and engaging multimedia content.

Engage with Your Audience: Foster engagement and interaction with your audience by responding to comments, messages, and inquiries promptly and courteously. Encourage feedback, questions, and discussions to create a sense of community and dialogue around your brand. Show appreciation for likes, shares, and mentions to build goodwill and loyalty among your followers.

Share Valuable Content: Share valuable and informative content that educates, entertains, or inspires your audience while showcasing your expertise and creativity. Share highlights of your work, case studies, tutorials, industry news, tips, and behind-the-scenes glimpses to provide value and keep your audience engaged. Use multimedia content such as videos, photos, infographics, and live streams to grab attention and stand out on social media.

Utilize Hashtags and Keywords: Use relevant hashtags, keywords, and tags in your social media posts to increase discoverability and reach a broader audience. Research trending hashtags and industry-specific keywords to incorporate into your content strategically. Participate in relevant conversations and join niche communities to expand your network and visibility on social media.

Collaborate with Influencers and Partners: Collaborate with influencers, brands, and industry partners to amplify your reach and exposure on social media. Partner with influencers or brand ambassadors to create sponsored content, host joint giveaways, or co-create engaging campaigns that reach their followers and expand your audience. Leverage partnerships and collaborations to tap into new networks and gain credibility within your industry.

Monitor and Analyze Performance: Monitor the performance of your online platforms and social media efforts using analytics tools and insights provided by each platform. Track metrics such as engagement, reach, impressions, clicks, and conversions to assess the effectiveness of your strategies and identify areas for improvement. Use data-driven insights to refine your approach, optimize content, and allocate resources more effectively.

By effectively utilizing online platforms and social media, you can amplify your brand presence, connect with your target audience, and generate leads and opportunities for your video production business. Stay active, authentic, and responsive on social media, and consistently provide value to your audience to build trust and loyalty over time.

Pitching Your Services to Potential Clients

Pitching your services to potential clients is a critical aspect of winning new business and growing your video production company. Here's how to craft an effective pitch:

Understand Client Needs: Research your potential clients thoroughly to understand their business, industry, goals, and challenges. Identify their specific needs, pain points, and objectives related to video production. Tailor your pitch to address their unique requirements and demonstrate how your services can solve their problems and help them achieve their goals.

Highlight Your Expertise: Showcase your expertise, experience, and track record in video production to establish credibility and trust with potential clients. Highlight relevant projects, case studies, client testimonials, and awards that demonstrate your capabilities and success in delivering high-quality video content. Emphasize your unique selling points, such as your creative approach, technical skills, and industry knowledge.

Customize Your Pitch: Customize your pitch to resonate with each potential client and align with their preferences, preferences, and priorities. Personalize your message to address the specific needs, concerns, and interests of the client. Use language, examples, and references that are relevant and relatable to the client's industry, audience, and objectives.

Articulate Value Proposition: Clearly articulate the value proposition of your video production services and how they can benefit the client. Highlight the key benefits, outcomes, and advantages of working with your company, such as increased brand awareness, engagement, conversions, or ROI. Demonstrate how your services can deliver tangible results and create value for the client's business.

Provide Solutions: Present tailored solutions and recommendations that address the client's needs and objectives effectively. Propose creative concepts, strategies, and approaches that demonstrate your understanding of the client's goals and challenges. Offer insights, ideas, and suggestions that showcase your ability to deliver innovative and impactful video content.

Offer Competitive Pricing: Present transparent and competitive pricing options that align with the client's budget and expectations. Provide detailed pricing packages or estimates that clearly outline the scope of work, deliverables, and costs associated with each service. Offer flexible pricing options or customizable packages to accommodate the client's budget constraints and preferences.

Showcase Portfolio: Showcase samples of your previous work, portfolio, and demo reels that highlight your creative abilities, production quality, and versatility. Select examples that are relevant to the client's industry, audience, and objectives to demonstrate your ability to deliver compelling and effective video content. Provide links to online portfolios, show-reels, or case studies for easy reference.

Engage and Follow Up: Engage the client in a meaningful conversation during the pitch meeting to address any questions, concerns, or objections they may have. Listen attentively to their feedback and respond promptly and professionally to build rapport and trust. Follow up after the pitch meeting to reiterate your interest, answer any additional questions, and solidify your relationship with the client.

Crafting a compelling and customized pitch that addresses the specific needs and objectives of potential clients, you can increase your chances of winning new business and establishing long-term relationships with clients in the video production industry. Tailor your message, showcase your expertise, and demonstrate the value of your services to position your company as the ideal partner for their video production needs.

Establishing Long-term Client Relationships

Establishing long-term client relationships is crucial for the success and sustainability of your video production company.

Here are strategies to foster lasting partnerships with your clients:

1. Understand Client Needs: Take the time to understand your clients' goals, objectives, and challenges thoroughly. Listen attentively to their requirements, preferences, and feedback to gain insights into their vision and expectations. Tailor your solutions and services to meet their specific needs and add value to their business.

2. Provide Exceptional Service: Strive to deliver exceptional service and exceed client expectations at every opportunity. Maintain open lines of communication, respond promptly to inquiries and requests, and demonstrate professionalism and reliability in all your interactions. Anticipate client needs and proactively address any issues or concerns that may arise during the project.

3. Consistent Quality and Reliability: Consistently deliver high-quality work that reflects your expertise, creativity, and attention to detail. Meet deadlines, adhere to project specifications, and ensure accuracy and consistency in your deliverables. Build a reputation for reliability, trustworthiness, and consistency in delivering outstanding results for your clients.

4. Foster Trust and Transparency: Build trust and transparency with your clients by being honest, upfront, and transparent in your communication and business practices. Provide clear and accurate estimates, timelines, and expectations from the outset of the project. Keep clients informed of progress, updates, and any changes that may impact the project's timeline or scope.

5. Be Responsive and Accessible: Make yourself accessible and responsive to your clients' needs, questions, and concerns throughout the duration of the project. Maintain open lines of communication through various channels, such as phone, email, or project management tools. Be proactive in addressing client inquiries, providing updates, and seeking feedback to ensure client satisfaction.

6. Demonstrate Value and Expertise: Continuously demonstrate the value of your services and expertise by delivering results that align with your clients' goals and objectives. Showcase your creativity, technical skills, and industry knowledge through your work and interactions with clients. Share insights, recommendations, and best practices to help clients achieve their business objectives.

7. Nurture Long-term Relationships: Invest in building long-term relationships with your clients beyond the completion of individual projects. Stay connected with clients through regular check-ins, updates, and follow-up communications. Celebrate milestones, anniversaries, and achievements together to reinforce the partnership and show appreciation for their continued support.

8. Seek Feedback and Iterate: Solicit feedback from your clients regularly to assess their satisfaction, gather insights, and identify areas for improvement. Actively listen to client feedback and take constructive criticism as an opportunity for growth and learning. Use client feedback to iterate and refine your processes, services, and offerings to better meet their needs and expectations.

9. Offer Value-added Services: Explore opportunities to offer value-added services or additional solutions that complement your core video production services. Provide strategic advice, creative brainstorming sessions, or post-production enhancements to enhance the overall value proposition for your clients. Anticipate emerging trends and technologies to offer innovative solutions that keep your clients ahead of the curve.

PROJECT MANAGEMENT

Project management plays a crucial role in the success and efficiency of video production projects. It involves coordinating various elements of the production process, from initial concept development to final delivery, to ensure that projects are completed on time, within budget, and to the client's satisfaction.

Effective project management begins with careful planning and organization. This includes defining project objectives, establishing timelines and milestones, allocating resources, and creating a detailed project plan. Project managers must also identify potential risks and develop contingency plans to mitigate them.

Communication is essential in project management, both within the production team and with clients. Project managers must facilitate clear and open communication among team members, ensuring that everyone understands their roles and responsibilities and that progress is tracked and documented effectively. Regular meetings and updates help keep the project on track and allow for timely adjustments as needed.

Budget management is another critical aspect of project management in video production. Project managers must track expenses, monitor budgets, and ensure that projects are completed within the allocated budget. This may involve negotiating with vendors, managing contracts, and finding creative solutions to minimize costs without compromising quality.

Quality control is essential to delivering successful video production projects. Project managers must oversee every stage of the production process, from scriptwriting and pre-production to filming and post-production, to ensure that the final product meets the client's expectations and quality standards. This may involve reviewing drafts, providing feedback, and coordinating revisions to ensure that the final product aligns with the client's vision.

Finally, project managers must evaluate the success of each project upon completion. This involves gathering feedback from clients and team members, assessing performance against project objectives and metrics, and identifying lessons learned for future projects. By continuously improving processes and practices, project managers can ensure that their video production projects are consistently successful and deliver value to clients.

Planning and Scheduling Shoots

Planning and scheduling shoots is a critical aspect of video production that requires careful coordination and organization to ensure successful outcomes. It involves determining the logistics, resources, and timelines required for each shoot to capture the desired footage efficiently and effectively.

The first step in planning and scheduling shoots is to define the scope and objectives of the project. This includes identifying the specific shots, scenes, and locations required to bring the script or concept to life. Collaborate closely with the creative team, clients, and stakeholders to clarify expectations, goals, and logistical considerations for each shoot.

Once the scope of the shoot is defined, create a detailed shooting schedule that outlines the timing, location, equipment, and personnel needed for each shoot day. Consider factors such as weather conditions, permit requirements, travel time, and equipment availability when scheduling shoots to minimize disruptions and maximize efficiency.

Coordinate with key personnel, including directors, cinematographers, production assistants, and talent, to confirm availability and roles for each shoot day. Ensure that all necessary equipment, props, wardrobe, and technical resources are secured and ready for use on set.

Communicate the shooting schedule and logistical details to all stakeholders involved, including crew members, talent, clients, and vendors. Provide clear instructions, call times, and contact information to ensure that everyone is informed and prepared for their roles and responsibilities.

During the shoot, closely monitor the progress and adhere to the schedule as closely as possible. Anticipate potential challenges or delays and make adjustments as needed to keep the production on track. Maintain open communication with the team and stakeholders to address any issues or concerns promptly.

After each shoot day, review the footage, assess the progress, and make any necessary adjustments to the schedule or production plan. Ensure that all necessary shots are captured, and any issues or gaps are addressed before moving on to the next phase of production.

Managing Resources and Logistics

Managing resources and logistics is essential for ensuring the smooth execution of video production projects. It involves coordinating various elements, including equipment, personnel, locations, and schedules, to optimize efficiency and achieve project goals within budget and timeline constraints.

Firstly, assess the resources needed for each project, including camera equipment, lighting gear, props, costumes, and talent. Create a comprehensive inventory of all required resources and identify any additional items or services that may be necessary to fulfill project requirements.

Next, allocate resources efficiently based on project priorities, timelines, and budget constraints. Determine the optimal use of equipment, personnel, and other resources to maximize productivity and minimize waste. Consider factors such as equipment availability, crew availability, and project deadlines when making resource allocation decisions.

Coordinate logistics such as transportation, accommodation, and permits to ensure smooth operations during filming. Arrange for transportation of equipment and crew to and from shoot locations, book accommodation for out-of-town shoots, and obtain necessary permits and permissions for filming in public or private locations.

Communicate logistics details and instructions clearly to all team members and stakeholders involved in the project. Provide call times, location details, and any specific requirements or instructions to ensure that everyone is informed and prepared for their roles and responsibilities.

Monitor resource usage and expenses closely throughout the project to stay within budget and identify any potential issues or inefficiencies. Track equipment rentals, personnel hours, and other expenses to ensure that costs are managed effectively and transparently.

Anticipate and address any potential logistical challenges or obstacles that may arise during the project. Develop contingency plans and alternative solutions to mitigate risks and minimize disruptions to the production schedule.

Maintain open communication with the production team, clients, vendors, and other stakeholders throughout the project to address any issues or concerns promptly. Encourage collaboration, teamwork, and problem-solving to overcome logistical challenges and ensure the successful completion of the project.

By effectively managing resources and logistics, you can optimize efficiency, minimize costs, and ensure the smooth execution of video production projects from start to finish. Prioritize organization, communication, and attention to detail to streamline operations and deliver high-quality results for your clients.

Overseeing Production and Post-Production Processes

Overseeing production and post-production processes is crucial for ensuring the successful execution of video production projects from start to finish. This involves managing various aspects of the production workflow, including filming, editing, and finalizing the video content, to deliver high-quality results that meet client expectations and project requirements.

During the production phase, oversee the filming process to ensure that all shots are captured according to the script, storyboard, and creative vision. Coordinate with the director, cinematographer, and production team to maintain consistency in lighting, framing, and composition throughout the shoot. Monitor the progress of the production schedule and address any issues or delays promptly to keep the project on track.

Provide direction and guidance to the production team, including camera operators, sound technicians, and production assistants, to ensure that everyone understands their roles and responsibilities.

Foster a collaborative and supportive work environment where team members can contribute their ideas and creativity to enhance the production process.

After filming is complete, transition to the post-production phase, where the raw footage is edited, processed, and refined to create the final video product. Oversee the editing process to ensure that the video content aligns with the client's vision, objectives, and quality standards. Work closely with the editor, colorist, and sound designer to review drafts, provide feedback, and make revisions as needed to achieve the desired outcome.

Manage the post-production timeline and workflow to ensure that deadlines are met and deliverables are completed on schedule. Coordinate with external vendors or subcontractors, such as visual effects studios or audio post-production facilities, to integrate additional elements or enhancements into the final video product.

Throughout the production and post-production processes, maintain open communication with clients, stakeholders, and team members to provide updates, gather feedback, and address any concerns or revisions. Solicit input from clients and incorporate their feedback into the creative process to ensure that the final product meets their expectations and objectives.

Oversee the delivery and distribution of the final video product to the client or intended audience through appropriate channels, such as online platforms, broadcast television, or live events. Ensure that all technical specifications, formats, and delivery requirements are met to ensure a seamless and successful handover of the completed project.

Ensuring Quality Control

Ensuring quality control is essential throughout every stage of the video production process to deliver high-quality results that meet client expectations and project requirements.

Here are key strategies to maintain quality control:

1. Establish Standards: Define clear quality standards and expectations for each project, including technical specifications, creative guidelines, and client preferences. Communicate these standards to the production team and stakeholders to ensure alignment and consistency in the final product.

2. Pre-Production Review: Conduct thorough reviews and approvals during the pre-production phase to ensure that scripts, storyboards, and creative concepts meet the client's objectives and vision.

Address any discrepancies or concerns early on to prevent issues from arising later in the production process.

3. On-Set Supervision: Maintain oversight and supervision during filming to ensure that shots are captured according to the established standards and creative direction. Monitor lighting, framing, composition, and performance to maintain consistency and continuity throughout the shoot.

4. Post-Production Review: Review rough cuts, edits, and drafts during the post-production phase to assess the quality of the footage, audio, and visual elements. Evaluate pacing, storytelling, transitions, and technical aspects to identify areas for improvement and refinement.

5. Technical Checks: Conduct technical checks and quality assessments of the video content to ensure that it meets industry standards and specifications. Verify video resolution, aspect ratio, color accuracy, audio levels, and file formats to ensure compatibility and compliance with delivery requirements.

6. Client Feedback: Solicit feedback from clients and stakeholders throughout the production process to gauge satisfaction and address any concerns or revisions promptly. Incorporate client feedback into the creative process to ensure that the final product aligns with their expectations and objectives.

7. Peer Review: Encourage peer review and collaboration among team members to identify and address potential issues or discrepancies in the production process. Foster a culture of constructive feedback and continuous improvement to enhance the overall quality of the work.

8. Final Quality Assurance: Conduct a final quality assurance review before delivering the completed project to the client. Verify that all elements meet the agreed-upon standards and specifications, and address any remaining issues or errors to ensure a polished and professional final product.

9. Continuous Improvement: Evaluate project outcomes and performance metrics to identify lessons learned and areas for improvement. Implement feedback mechanisms, process improvements, and training initiatives to enhance quality control practices and optimize future projects.

MARKETING AND BRANDING

Marketing and branding are essential components of building a successful video production company. Effective marketing and branding strategies help to create awareness, attract clients, and differentiate your company from competitors in the industry.

Marketing involves promoting your services and capabilities to potential clients through various channels and tactics. This includes developing a strong online presence through your website, social media platforms, and online advertising. Utilize search engine optimization (SEO) techniques to improve your website's visibility in search engine results and attract organic traffic. Engage with your audience on social media by sharing engaging content, behind-the-scenes glimpses, and client testimonials to showcase your expertise and build credibility.

In addition to online marketing, explore offline marketing channels such as networking events, industry conferences, and trade shows to connect with potential clients and industry professionals. Participate in speaking engagements, workshops, and panel discussions to position yourself as an authority in the field and increase visibility for your company.

Branding plays a crucial role in shaping the identity and perception of your video production company. Develop a strong brand identity that reflects your company's values, personality, and unique selling proposition. This includes creating a memorable logo, color palette, and visual style that resonate with your target audience and convey professionalism and creativity.

Consistency is key to effective branding. Ensure that your brand messaging, imagery, and tone of voice are consistent across all marketing materials and communication channels. This helps to build brand recognition and reinforce your company's identity in the minds of clients and prospects.

Focus on building relationships and providing value to your clients through exceptional service and memorable experiences. Foster positive word-of-mouth referrals and testimonials from satisfied clients by delivering high-quality work and exceeding expectations.

Stay informed about industry trends, emerging technologies, and evolving client preferences to adapt your marketing and branding strategies accordingly. Continuously monitor and analyze the performance of your marketing efforts to identify areas for improvement and optimize your approach over time.

Prioritize building a strong brand identity, engaging with your audience, and delivering exceptional value to clients to drive growth and success for your business.

Developing a Strong Brand Identity

Developing a strong brand identity is essential for establishing a distinct and memorable presence in the video production industry. A strong brand identity helps to convey your company's values, personality, and unique selling proposition to clients and prospects. Here's how to develop a strong brand identity for your video production company:

Define Your Brand Values and Mission: Start by defining the core values and mission of your company. What principles guide your business? What do you aspire to achieve? Your brand values and mission should reflect your commitment to quality, creativity, innovation, and client satisfaction.

Identify Your Target Audience: Understand who your target audience is and what they value. What are their demographics, interests, and preferences? Tailor your brand identity to resonate with your target audience and address their needs and aspirations.

Create a Memorable Logo and Visual Identity: Design a distinctive logo and visual identity that represents your brand effectively. Your logo should be visually appealing, memorable, and reflective of your company's personality and values. Consider colors, typography, and imagery that evoke the desired emotions and perceptions associated with your brand.

Craft a Compelling Brand Story: Develop a compelling brand story that communicates the essence of your company and resonates with your audience. Highlight your company's history, values, and unique selling points in a way that engages and captivates your audience.

Consistency is Key: Maintain consistency in your brand identity across all touchpoints and communication channels. Ensure that your logo, colors, typography, and messaging are consistent in your website, social media profiles, marketing materials, and client interactions. Consistency helps to build brand recognition and trust with your audience.

Deliver Exceptional Experiences: Your brand identity is not just about visual elements—it's also about the experiences you deliver to your clients. Focus on providing exceptional service, quality work, and memorable experiences that align with your brand values and leave a lasting impression on your clients.

Engage with Your Audience: Build relationships with your audience through meaningful engagement and interaction. Listen to their feedback, respond to their inquiries, and provide valuable content and insights that demonstrate your expertise and commitment to their success.

Stay True to Your Brand: Stay true to your brand identity and values, even as your business evolves and grows. Be authentic, transparent, and consistent in your messaging and actions, and ensure that every aspect of your business reflects your brand identity.

Creating a Portfolio of Work

Creating a portfolio of work is essential for showcasing your skills, expertise, and creativity as a video production company. Your portfolio serves as a visual representation of your capabilities and helps potential clients understand the quality and style of your work.

Here's how to create a compelling portfolio of work:

Select Your Best Work: Choose a selection of your best projects to include in your portfolio. Focus on showcasing a diverse range of work that demonstrates your versatility, creativity, and ability to meet different client needs. Highlight projects that align with your target audience and showcase your strengths as a video production company.

Organize Your Portfolio: Organize your portfolio in a logical and visually appealing manner. Consider grouping projects by category, industry, or type of video (e.g., commercials, corporate videos, documentaries) to make it easy for viewers to navigate and find relevant examples of your work. Use clear and concise titles and descriptions to provide context for each project.

Showcase Variety and Depth: Include a variety of projects that highlight different aspects of your capabilities, such as storytelling, cinematography, editing, and visual effects. Showcase projects of varying scales, budgets, and production styles to demonstrate your adaptability and versatility as a video production company. Aim to provide depth and breadth in your portfolio to appeal to a wide range of clients.

Focus on Quality: Prioritize quality over quantity when selecting projects for your portfolio. Choose projects that showcase your best work in terms of production value, creativity, and client satisfaction. Ensure that the videos you include are well-produced, visually compelling, and effectively communicate the intended message or story.

Provide Context and Details: Include relevant information and details about each project in your portfolio. Provide a brief overview of the project objectives, client goals, and your role in the production process. Highlight any challenges, creative solutions, or unique aspects of the project that demonstrate your problem-solving skills and ingenuity.

Use Multimedia Elements: Incorporate multimedia elements such as video clips, images, and testimonials to enhance your portfolio and engage viewers. Include behind-the-scenes footage, production stills, or before-and-after examples to provide insight into your creative process and attention to detail. Incorporate client testimonials or reviews to add credibility and social proof to your portfolio.

Keep it updated: Regularly update your portfolio with new projects and remove outdated or irrelevant content. As you complete new projects, add them to your portfolio to keep it fresh and showcase your latest work. Consider periodically refreshing the design and layout of your portfolio to maintain visual appeal and relevance.

Share Your Portfolio: Make your portfolio easily accessible and shareable across various platforms, including your website, social media profiles, and email signature. Consider creating a digital portfolio or show-reel that you can share with potential clients during meetings, pitches, or networking events.

Implementing Digital Marketing Strategies (e.g., SEO, Content Marketing)

Implementing digital marketing strategies is essential for promoting your video production company, attracting clients, and growing your business online. Here are key digital marketing strategies to consider:

Search Engine Optimization (SEO): Optimize your website and online content to improve visibility in search engine results pages (SERPs). Conduct keyword research to identify relevant search terms and incorporate them into your website content, meta tags, and URLs. Optimize your website's technical aspects, such as page speed, mobile-friendliness, and site structure, to enhance user experience and search engine rankings.

Content Marketing: Create high-quality, informative, and engaging content that resonates with your target audience and showcases your expertise in video production. Publish blog posts, articles, case studies, and how-to guides that address common questions, challenges, and trends in the industry. Share valuable insights, tips, and best practices to attract and engage your audience and position your company as a thought leader in the field.

Social Media Marketing: Leverage social media platforms such as Facebook, Instagram, Twitter, LinkedIn, and YouTube to connect with your audience, share content, and promote your video production services. Create a content calendar and post regularly to keep your audience engaged and informed. Use multimedia content such as videos, photos, and infographics to grab attention and showcase your work.

Email Marketing: Build an email list of prospects, clients, and industry contacts and use email marketing campaigns to nurture leads, promote your services, and drive conversions. Send targeted, personalized email campaigns that provide value to your subscribers, such as exclusive offers, industry insights, and behind-the-scenes updates. Use email automation tools to streamline the process and deliver relevant content to your audience.

Pay-Per-Click (PPC) Advertising: Run targeted PPC advertising campaigns on platforms such as Google Ads and social media channels to reach potential clients and drive website traffic. Create compelling ad copy and landing pages that resonate with your target audience and encourage action. Monitor campaign performance, adjust bids and targeting settings, and optimize ad copy to maximize ROI and achieve your advertising goals.

Video Marketing: Harness the power of video marketing to promote your video production services and showcase your work. Create engaging video content that highlights your capabilities, showcases your portfolio, and provides value to your audience. Share your videos on your website, social media channels, and video-sharing platforms to increase visibility and attract potential clients.

Analytics and Measurement: Track and analyze the performance of your digital marketing efforts using web analytics tools such as Google Analytics. Monitor key metrics such as website traffic, engagement, conversions, and ROI to evaluate the effectiveness of your strategies and identify areas for improvement. Use data-driven insights to refine your approach, optimize campaigns, and allocate resources more effectively.

Leveraging Testimonials and Case Studies

Leveraging testimonials and case studies is a powerful marketing strategy for establishing credibility, building trust, and attracting new clients to your video production company. Here's how to effectively leverage testimonials and case studies in your marketing efforts:

Testimonials:

Collect testimonials from satisfied clients who have worked with your company in the past. Reach out to clients after completing a project and request feedback on their experience working with your team.

Highlight positive comments, reviews, and endorsements from clients on your website, social media profiles, and marketing materials. Use compelling quotes and testimonials that showcase the value and impact of your services.

Include testimonials on relevant pages of your website, such as your homepage, services page, and portfolio section. Display testimonials prominently and prominently to catch the attention of visitors and reinforce your credibility.

Consider creating a dedicated testimonials page on your website where visitors can read reviews and testimonials from satisfied clients. Organize testimonials by project type, industry, or client category to make it easy for visitors to find relevant examples.

Encourage clients to leave reviews and testimonials on third-party review platforms such as Google My Business, Yelp, and industry-specific directories. Positive reviews and ratings can boost your credibility and help attract new clients.

Case Studies:

Develop case studies that showcase your company's capabilities, expertise, and successful projects. Highlight specific challenges, objectives, and solutions for each case study to provide insight into your process and results.

Choose case studies that demonstrate your ability to solve common problems or address industry-specific challenges. Showcase a variety of projects to appeal to different client needs and preferences.

Include key metrics, results, and outcomes in your case studies to demonstrate the effectiveness and impact of your services. Use data-driven insights to quantify the success of your projects and illustrate the value you provide to clients.

Share case studies on your website, blog, social media channels, and email newsletters to reach a wider audience. Use engaging visuals, multimedia content, and storytelling techniques to make your case studies more compelling and memorable.

Consider creating video case studies or client testimonials that feature interviews with clients and highlight the story behind the project. Video content can be highly engaging and persuasive, making it an effective way to showcase your work and connect with potential clients.

By leveraging testimonials and case studies effectively, you can build credibility, establish trust, and attract new clients to your video production company. Incorporate testimonials and case studies into your marketing strategy to showcase your expertise, highlight your success stories, and differentiate your company from competitors.

SCALING YOUR BUSINESS

Scaling your video production business involves growing your operations, expanding your client base, and increasing your revenue while maintaining quality and efficiency.

Here are key strategies for scaling your business:

1. Streamline Processes: Identify areas of inefficiency in your production process and streamline workflows to improve productivity and reduce costs. Implement project management tools, automation software, and standardized procedures to streamline tasks, optimize resource allocation, and enhance collaboration among team members.

2. Invest in Technology: Invest in advanced video production equipment, software, and technology to enhance the quality and efficiency of your productions. Upgrade your cameras, editing software, and post-production tools to stay competitive and meet client demands for high-quality content.

3. Expand Service Offerings: Diversify your service offerings to cater to a broader range of client needs and preferences. Consider offering additional services such as live streaming, virtual reality

(VR) production, animation, or aerial drone footage to attract new clients and increase revenue streams.

4. Hire and Train Talent: Expand your team by hiring skilled professionals with expertise in video production, cinematography, editing, and other relevant areas. Invest in training and professional development programs to develop the skills and capabilities of your team members and ensure that they stay up-to-date with industry trends and best practices.

5. Develop Strategic Partnerships: Collaborate with other professionals and companies in related industries, such as marketing agencies, event planners, or digital media firms, to expand your network and reach new clients. Develop strategic partnerships and referral programs to leverage each other's expertise, resources, and networks for mutual benefit.

6. Scale Marketing Efforts: Increase your marketing efforts to raise awareness of your brand and attract new clients. Invest in digital marketing strategies such as search engine optimization (SEO), content marketing, social media advertising, and email marketing to reach your target audience and generate leads.

7. Improve Client Relationships: Focus on building strong, long-term relationships with your clients by delivering exceptional service, exceeding expectations, and providing ongoing support and

communication. Prioritize client satisfaction and loyalty to generate repeat business, referrals, and positive reviews that contribute to business growth.

8. Monitor Performance Metrics: Track key performance metrics such as revenue, profitability, client acquisition costs, and customer satisfaction to assess the effectiveness of your scaling efforts. Use data-driven insights to identify areas for improvement, make informed decisions, and adjust your strategies as needed to achieve your business goals.

9. Plan for Scalability: Anticipate future growth and plan for scalability by investing in scalable infrastructure, systems, and resources that can accommodate increasing demand and workload. Develop a clear roadmap and growth strategy that outlines your objectives, milestones, and action plans for scaling your business over time.

Expanding Service Offerings (e.g., Live Streaming, Animation)

Expanding your service offerings can be a strategic move to diversify your video production business and attract a wider range of clients. By offering additional services beyond traditional video production, you can tap into new markets, meet evolving client needs, and increase revenue streams.

One area to consider expanding into is live streaming services. With the rise of online events, webinars, and virtual meetings, there is a growing demand for live streaming solutions. By offering live streaming services, you can help clients reach broader audiences, engage with their viewers in real-time, and deliver dynamic and interactive content. Whether it's live events, product launches, or corporate meetings, live streaming can add value to your service offerings and enhance your client's online presence.

Animation is another area ripe for expansion. Animated videos can be highly effective for explaining complex concepts, storytelling, and engaging audiences across various platforms. By offering animation services, you can cater to clients looking to create captivating and visually appealing content for their marketing campaigns, explainer videos, training materials, and more. Whether it's 2D animation, 3D animation, or motion graphics, adding animation to your repertoire can broaden your creative capabilities and attract clients seeking innovative and engaging video content.

Additionally, consider expanding into emerging technologies such as virtual reality (VR) production and augmented reality (AR) experiences. VR and AR offer immersive and interactive storytelling opportunities that can captivate audiences and provide unique brand experiences. By offering VR and AR production services, you can position your company at the forefront of innovation and help clients create memorable and impactful experiences for their target audiences.

Other potential service offerings to explore include drone videography and photography, which can provide stunning aerial footage for various applications such as real estate, tourism, events, and more. Additionally, offering video editing and post-production services as standalone offerings can cater to clients who have their own footage but lack the expertise or resources to edit and polish it to professional standards.

Expanding your service offerings requires careful consideration of market demand, client preferences, and your company's capabilities. Conduct market research, assess your resources and expertise, and strategically invest in training, equipment, and talent to support your expansion into new service areas. By diversifying your service offerings, you can position your video production business for growth and success in a competitive and evolving industry landscape.

Scaling Operations and Infrastructure

Scaling operations and infrastructure is crucial for managing growth, increasing efficiency, and maintaining quality as your video production business expands.

Here are key strategies for scaling operations and infrastructure:

1. Invest in Technology: Upgrade your production equipment, software, and technology to improve efficiency, enhance capabilities, and meet growing demand. Invest in high-quality cameras, lighting equipment, editing software, and post-production tools to streamline workflows and deliver professional-grade video content.

2. Expand Physical Infrastructure: Evaluate your studio space, office facilities, and production facilities to accommodate increased production volume and staff. Consider expanding your physical infrastructure or relocating to a larger space if necessary to support growth. Invest in studio upgrades, set designs, and equipment storage solutions to optimize your production environment.

3. Automate and Standardize Processes: Implement automation tools, standardized workflows, and production templates to streamline operations and minimize manual tasks. Use project management software, scheduling tools, and collaboration platforms to coordinate tasks, track progress, and communicate effectively across teams.

4. Scale Workforce and Talent: Hire additional staff and talent to support increased production volume and expanded service offerings. Recruit skilled professionals in areas such as cinematography, editing, animation, and post-production to enhance your capabilities and meet client demands. Invest in training and professional development programs to develop the skills and expertise of your team members.

5. Develop Strategic Partnerships: Forge strategic partnerships and alliances with other industry professionals, vendors, and service providers to complement your capabilities and scale your operations. Collaborate with freelance professionals, subcontractors, or specialized agencies to augment your workforce and resources as needed for specific projects or client needs.

6. Implement Quality Assurance Measures: Establish quality assurance processes and standards to maintain consistency, accuracy, and excellence in your productions as you scale. Implement quality control checks, peer reviews, and client feedback mechanisms to monitor and improve the quality of your work and ensure client satisfaction.

7. Enhance Customer Support and Service: Invest in customer support systems, client communication channels, and client management tools to enhance the client experience and support increased client interactions as your business grows. Provide responsive, personalized, and proactive customer service to build long-term relationships and foster client loyalty.

8. Monitor Performance and Metrics: Track key performance indicators (KPIs), production metrics, and operational data to assess the performance of your operations and infrastructure. Monitor metrics such as production efficiency, turnaround times, resource utilization, and client satisfaction to identify areas for improvement and optimize your processes.

9. Plan for Scalability: Anticipate future growth and plan for scalability by designing flexible, scalable infrastructure and operations that can accommodate increasing demand and workload. Consider cloud-based solutions, scalable software platforms, and modular production setups that can easily adapt to changing requirements and scale with your business.

Diversifying Revenue Streams

Diversifying revenue streams is a strategic approach to strengthen the financial stability and sustainability of your video production business. By expanding your sources of income beyond traditional video production services, you can mitigate risks, capitalize on new opportunities, and create multiple streams of revenue.

Here are several strategies for diversifying revenue streams:

1. Offer Additional Services: Expand your service offerings to include complementary services that align with your core competencies and client needs. Consider offering services such as photography, graphic design, content marketing, social media management, or website development to provide clients with comprehensive solutions and increase revenue opportunities.

2. Develop Product Lines: Create and sell digital products or merchandise related to video production, such as stock footage, stock music, motion graphics templates, or video editing presets. Develop branded merchandise such as apparel, accessories, or merchandise featuring your company logo or creative designs to generate additional revenue and strengthen brand visibility.

3. Monetize Intellectual Property: Capitalize on your creative assets and intellectual property by licensing or selling rights to your video content, footage, or creative concepts. Explore opportunities to monetize your content through licensing agreements, syndication deals, or partnerships with media outlets, content platforms, or distribution networks.

4. Offer Training and Education: Leverage your expertise and experience in video production to offer training, workshops, or educational resources for aspiring filmmakers, content creators, or industry professionals. Develop online courses, tutorials, or masterclasses covering topics such as video production techniques, editing skills, storytelling, or business fundamentals to generate revenue and establish your company as a knowledge leader in the industry.

5. Provide Consulting Services: Offer consulting services to businesses, organizations, or individuals seeking guidance and expertise in video production, content strategy, or digital marketing. Provide strategic advice, creative direction, or project management support to help clients achieve their video production goals and maximize the effectiveness of their video content.

6. Explore Sponsorships and Partnerships: Collaborate with brands, sponsors, or advertisers to create sponsored content, branded videos, or integrated marketing campaigns. Partner with companies seeking to reach your audience through product placements, endorsements, or co-branded content initiatives. Explore opportunities for affiliate marketing or revenue-sharing agreements to monetize content and generate additional income.

7. Generate Passive Income: Create passive income streams by monetizing digital assets, such as online courses, e-books, templates, or subscription-based services. Develop premium content offerings, membership programs, or subscription models that provide recurring revenue streams and passive income opportunities for your business.

8. Invest in Real Estate or Equipment Rental: Diversify your revenue streams by investing in real estate properties or equipment rental services related to video production. Purchase studio space, production facilities, or equipment inventory and generate rental income by leasing out space or equipment to other filmmakers, production companies, or creatives.

Evaluating Growth Opportunities

Evaluating growth opportunities is essential for identifying areas of potential expansion and maximizing the growth potential of your video production business.

Here are key steps for evaluating growth opportunities:

1. Conduct Market Research: Start by conducting comprehensive market research to identify emerging trends, market dynamics, and growth opportunities in the video production industry. Analyze industry reports, market data, and competitor analysis to gain insights into market demand, client preferences, and competitive landscape.

2. Assess Client Needs and Preferences: Understand the evolving needs, preferences, and challenges of your target audience and client base. Gather feedback from clients, conduct surveys, and analyze customer data to identify areas where your services can add value and address unmet needs or pain points.

3. Identify Niche Markets: Explore niche markets or specialized segments within the video production industry where you can differentiate your services and capitalize on specific client needs or industry trends. Consider targeting niche markets such as healthcare, technology, education, or non-profit organizations that require specialized expertise or content solutions.

4. Evaluate Service Expansion: Assess opportunities to expand your service offerings or introduce new services that align with your core competencies and client demands. Consider adding services such as live streaming, animation, virtual reality (VR) production, or content marketing to diversify your revenue streams and meet evolving client needs.

5. Explore Geographic Expansion: Evaluate opportunities for geographic expansion or market penetration by targeting new regions, cities, or countries where there is demand for video production services. Consider establishing satellite offices, partnerships, or remote teams to extend your reach and serve clients in new markets effectively.

6. Leverage Technology and Innovation: Embrace emerging technologies and innovation to unlock new growth opportunities and stay ahead of the competition. Explore trends such as 360-degree video, augmented reality (AR), artificial intelligence (AI), or interactive video experiences that offer innovative ways to engage audiences and create impactful content.

7. Assess Strategic Partnerships: Identify potential strategic partnerships, collaborations, or alliances with other industry players, technology providers, or complementary businesses that can enhance your capabilities, expand your reach, or access new markets. Evaluate partnerships that align with your business objectives and provide mutual benefits for all parties involved.

8. Evaluate Financial Viability: Assess the financial viability and potential return on investment (ROI) of growth opportunities by conducting a cost-benefit analysis, revenue projections, and risk assessment. Evaluate factors such as upfront investment costs, revenue potential, market demand, and competitive landscape to determine the feasibility and profitability of each growth opportunity.

9. Prioritize Growth Initiatives: Prioritize growth opportunities based on their strategic alignment, market potential, resource requirements, and growth objectives. Focus on initiatives that offer the greatest potential for long-term success and sustainable growth while aligning with your company's vision, mission, and values.

Continuously monitor market trends, client feedback, and industry developments to identify new growth opportunities and adapt your growth strategy to capitalize on changing market dynamics and emerging trends.

MAINTAINING SUCCESS AND SUSTAINABILITY

Maintaining success and sustainability is essential for the long-term viability and growth of your video production business.

Here are key strategies to ensure continued success and sustainability:

Continuous Improvement: Foster a culture of continuous improvement within your organization by encouraging innovation, learning, and adaptation. Invest in professional development, training programs, and skills enhancement initiatives to keep your team members motivated, engaged, and up-to-date with industry trends and best practices. Solicit feedback from clients, stakeholders, and team members to identify areas for improvement and implement changes to enhance the quality of your services and operations.

Client Satisfaction: Prioritize client satisfaction and retention by delivering exceptional service, exceeding expectations, and building strong, long-term relationships with your clients. Listen to client feedback, address their needs and concerns promptly, and go above and beyond to deliver value-added solutions and personalized experiences. Cultivate a reputation for reliability, professionalism, and integrity that inspires trust and loyalty among your clients.

Financial Management: Maintain sound financial management practices to ensure the financial health and stability of your business. Implement budgeting, forecasting, and financial planning processes to monitor and manage cash flow, expenses, and revenue streams effectively. Diversify your revenue streams, minimize debt, and build up reserves to weather economic uncertainties and unforeseen challenges.

Operational Efficiency: Streamline operations, optimize workflows, and leverage technology to improve efficiency and productivity across your organization. Automate repetitive tasks, standardize processes, and implement project management tools to streamline project delivery, minimize errors, and maximize resource utilization. Regularly assess and optimize your operations to eliminate bottlenecks, reduce costs, and enhance overall efficiency.

Quality Control: Maintain high standards of quality and excellence in your productions by implementing rigorous quality control measures and standards. Establish quality assurance processes, review checkpoints, and quality control checks at each stage of the production process to ensure consistency, accuracy, and adherence to client specifications and industry standards. Invest in training, equipment, and resources to uphold quality and deliver superior results to your clients.

Risk Management: Identify, assess, and mitigate risks to your business operations, projects, and reputation proactively. Conduct risk assessments, develop contingency plans, and implement risk mitigation strategies to minimize the impact of potential threats such as equipment failure, project delays, or client disputes. Stay informed about industry regulations, legal requirements, and best practices to ensure compliance and minimize legal and regulatory risks.

Community Engagement: Engage with your local community and industry networks to build relationships, foster goodwill, and contribute to the broader community. Participate in industry events, sponsorships, and charitable initiatives to raise your company's profile, demonstrate corporate social responsibility, and support causes aligned with your values and mission. Build partnerships and collaborations with local businesses, organizations, and community groups to create mutually beneficial opportunities for growth and collaboration.

Adaptability and Resilience: Adapt to changing market conditions, technological advancements, and client preferences by remaining flexible, agile, and resilient in your approach. Embrace innovation, embrace change, and be willing to pivot or evolve your business model, services, or strategies in response to shifting trends and opportunities. Anticipate future challenges and opportunities, and position your business to adapt and thrive in dynamic and uncertain environments.

Staying Updated with Industry Trends and Technology

Staying updated with industry trends and technology is essential for the success and competitiveness of your video production business. In today's fast-paced digital landscape, where technology and consumer preferences are constantly evolving, staying ahead of the curve is paramount.

To stay updated with industry trends, it's crucial to actively engage with industry publications, websites, blogs, and social media channels that specialize in video production, filmmaking, and digital media. Follow industry leaders, influencers, and experts on platforms like LinkedIn, Twitter, and YouTube to stay informed about the latest developments, insights, and best practices in the field.

Attending industry events, conferences, trade shows, and workshops is another effective way to stay updated with industry trends and network with other professionals in the field. These events provide opportunities to learn from industry experts, attend seminars and panel discussions, and discover new technologies, techniques, and innovations shaping the future of video production.

Joining professional associations, guilds, or online communities related to video production can also provide valuable networking opportunities and access to resources, training programs, and industry news. Engaging with peers, sharing knowledge and experiences, and participating in discussions can help you stay informed about emerging trends, challenges, and opportunities in the industry.

In addition to staying updated with industry trends, it's essential to keep abreast of advancements in technology that impact the video production process. Monitor developments in camera technology, editing software, visual effects tools, and post-production techniques to identify opportunities to improve efficiency, enhance quality, and offer new services to clients.

Investing in continuing education, training programs, and certifications can help you and your team members stay current with the latest technologies and techniques in video production. Many industry organizations, software vendors, and training providers offer courses, workshops, and certifications covering topics such as cinematography, editing, color grading, and virtual reality (VR) production.

Lastly, maintaining an open mindset, embracing experimentation, and being willing to adapt to change are essential attitudes for staying updated with industry trends and technology. Keep an eye on emerging trends, experiment with new tools and techniques, and be proactive in seeking out opportunities to innovate and differentiate your video production business in a competitive market.

Staying updated with industry trends and technology, you can position your video production business for long-term success, remain competitive in a rapidly changing landscape, and continue to deliver high-quality, innovative solutions to your clients.

Continuing Education and Skill Development

Continuing education and skill development are essential for professionals in the video production industry to stay relevant, competitive, and successful in their careers. In an industry that is constantly evolving with new technologies, techniques, and trends, ongoing learning is crucial for keeping up with the pace of change and expanding one's knowledge and expertise.

There are various avenues for continuing education and skill development in video production. One option is to pursue formal education and training programs offered by universities, colleges, and specialized institutions. These programs often provide comprehensive training in areas such as cinematography, editing, sound design, visual effects, and production management, and can lead to degrees, diplomas, or certifications.

Another option is to enroll in online courses, workshops, and tutorials offered by industry experts, training platforms, and software vendors. Online learning platforms such as LinkedIn Learning, Udemy, and Skillshare offer a wide range of courses covering various aspects of video production, from basic techniques to advanced skills and specialized topics such as motion graphics, color grading, and drone videography.

Additionally, attending industry events, conferences, and workshops can provide valuable opportunities for networking, learning, and skill development. These events often feature presentations, panel discussions, and hands-on workshops led by industry professionals, where attendees can learn about the latest trends, technologies, and best practices in video production.

Seeking mentorship and guidance from experienced professionals in the industry can be invaluable for skill development and career advancement. Mentors can provide guidance, feedback, and support, share their knowledge and expertise, and help mentees navigate challenges and opportunities in their careers.

Practicing and honing one's skills through hands-on experience is also essential for skill development in video production. Taking on projects, collaborating with peers, and experimenting with different techniques and tools can help professionals refine their craft, develop their style, and build a portfolio of work that showcases their talents and capabilities.

Finally, staying curious, proactive, and adaptable is crucial for continuous learning and skill development in the fast-paced world of video production. Professionals should stay updated with industry trends, technological advancements, and best practices, and be willing to embrace new challenges, experiment with new techniques, and push the boundaries of their creativity and expertise.

Investing in continuing education and skill development, professionals in the video production industry can enhance their capabilities, expand their opportunities, and stay competitive in an ever-changing and dynamic field. Continuing education is not just a one-time event but a lifelong journey of learning and growth that is essential for success and fulfillment in one's career.

Nurturing Client Relationships and Repeat Business

Nurturing client relationships and fostering repeat business is fundamental to the long-term success and sustainability of a video production business. Building strong, lasting relationships with clients not only leads to repeat business but also generates referrals, enhances brand reputation, and contributes to overall business growth.

To nurture client relationships and encourage repeat business, it's essential to prioritize communication, responsiveness, and client satisfaction throughout every stage of the project lifecycle. This involves:

1. Understanding Client Needs: Take the time to understand your clients' goals, preferences, and expectations for their video projects. Actively listen to their ideas, concerns, and feedback, and collaborate with them to develop solutions that align with their vision and objectives.

2. Clear Communication: Maintain open, transparent communication with clients throughout the project, providing regular updates on progress, timelines, and deliverables. Address any questions, concerns, or issues promptly and professionally, and keep clients informed of any changes or developments that may impact the project.

3. Providing Value-Added Service: Go above and beyond to exceed client expectations and deliver exceptional value with each project. Offer creative insights, strategic guidance, and personalized recommendations that demonstrate your expertise and commitment to helping clients achieve their goals.

4. Delivering High-Quality Work: Consistently deliver high-quality video content that meets or exceeds client expectations in terms of creativity, technical excellence, and storytelling. Pay attention to detail, adhere to project requirements, and strive for excellence in every aspect of the production process.

5. Building Trust and Credibility: Build trust and credibility with clients by consistently delivering on your promises, maintaining integrity and professionalism, and demonstrating reliability and accountability in your actions. Foster a collaborative and respectful working relationship based on mutual trust and respect.

6. Providing Exceptional Customer Service: Offer exceptional customer service and support throughout the client's journey, from initial inquiry to project completion and beyond. Be responsive to client inquiries, provide timely assistance and support, and ensure that clients feel valued and appreciated throughout their interactions with your company.

7. Seeking Feedback and Continuous Improvement: Solicit feedback from clients at the end of each project to gain insights into their experience and identify areas for improvement. Use client feedback to refine your processes, enhance service offerings, and address any issues or concerns to ensure ongoing client satisfaction and loyalty.

8. Maintaining Long-Term Relationships: Cultivate long-term relationships with clients by staying in touch, expressing appreciation for their business, and finding opportunities to add value over time. Keep clients informed of new services, promotions, or industry updates that may be relevant to their needs and interests.

Adapting to Changing Market Conditions

Adapting to changing market conditions is crucial for the success and sustainability of a video production business. In an industry that is constantly evolving due to technological advancements, shifting consumer preferences, and economic fluctuations, being adaptable and responsive to changes is essential to remain competitive and thrive.

Here's how video production businesses can adapt to changing market conditions:

1. Stay Informed: Keep abreast of industry trends, market dynamics, and emerging technologies by regularly monitoring industry publications, attending industry events, and networking with peers. Stay informed about changes in consumer behavior, market demand, and competitive landscape to anticipate shifts and proactively adjust your business strategies accordingly.

2. Flexibility and Agility: Cultivate a culture of flexibility and agility within your organization to quickly respond to changing market conditions and unforeseen challenges. Be willing to pivot your strategies, adapt your services, and explore new opportunities as market dynamics evolve.

3. Diversify Offerings: Diversify your service offerings to meet changing client needs and market demands. Explore new service

areas, such as live streaming, virtual reality (VR), or augmented reality (AR), to expand your capabilities and appeal to a broader range of clients. Consider offering bundled packages or customizable solutions to accommodate varying client preferences and budgets.

4. Embrace Technology: Embrace technological advancements and innovations to enhance your production capabilities, streamline workflows, and deliver high-quality results efficiently. Invest in cutting-edge equipment, software tools, and digital platforms that can help you stay competitive and meet the evolving demands of clients in a digital-first world.

5. Focus on Value: Shift your focus from solely delivering products to providing value-added solutions and experiences that address client pain points and deliver tangible results. Emphasize the value proposition of your services, such as creative expertise, technical excellence, and strategic insights, to differentiate your business and attract clients in a crowded market.

6. Customer-Centric Approach: Adopt a customer-centric approach to business operations, placing the needs and preferences of clients at the forefront of decision-making processes. Listen to client feedback, solicit input, and adapt your services to better align with client expectations and deliver superior experiences.

7. Strategic Partnerships: Forge strategic partnerships and collaborations with other industry players, technology providers, or complementary businesses to leverage each other's strengths and resources. Collaborate with partners to access new markets, share expertise, and capitalize on synergies that can enhance your competitive advantage and adaptability.

8. Monitor and Evaluate: Continuously monitor market trends, client feedback, and business performance metrics to assess the effectiveness of your strategies and identify areas for improvement. Use data-driven insights to make informed decisions, refine your approaches, and stay agile in response to changing market conditions.

CONCLUSION

In conclusion, starting and running a successful video production company requires careful planning, dedication, and adaptability to thrive in a competitive and ever-evolving industry landscape. From understanding the video production industry and market research to building a talented team, crafting a solid business plan, and delivering exceptional service to clients, every aspect of the business plays a crucial role in its success.

By staying informed about industry trends and technology, nurturing client relationships, adapting to changing market conditions, and maintaining a commitment to continuous learning and improvement, video production businesses can position themselves for long-term success and sustainability.

While challenges may arise along the way, embracing innovation, fostering creativity, and prioritizing client satisfaction can help video production companies overcome obstacles and achieve their goals. By remaining focused on delivering high-quality work, providing value-added solutions, and cultivating a reputation for excellence, video production businesses can build a loyal client base, drive revenue growth, and establish themselves as leaders in the industry.

Ultimately, success in the video production business is not just about creating compelling visuals or cutting-edge technology—it's about understanding clients' needs, delivering impactful storytelling, and building meaningful relationships that stand the test of time. With dedication, passion, and a commitment to excellence, video production companies can create lasting impact and leave a lasting legacy in the dynamic world of media and entertainment.

www.ingramcontent.com/pod-product-compliance
Lightning Source LLC
Chambersburg PA
CBHW071923210526
45479CB00002B/527